# Home schooling Methods

Seasoned Advice on Learning Styles

GENERAL EDITORS,

## Paul & Gena Suarez

B&H
PUBLISHING GROUP

NASHVILLE, TENNESSEE

This work is dedicated to Jesus Christ, our great God and Savior. Without him, we are nothing and can do nothing. And with him, we are chosen to receive his inheritance, his gift of eternal life. No words exist which can express fully our gratefulness for his sacrifice, his perfect Son.

# Contents

Acknowledgments     **ix**

Introduction     **1**

**Classical Education Method**     **3**

Classical and Christian Education by Douglas Wilson     **6**

What Is Classical Education? by Christine Miller     **13**

**Principle Approach Method**     **27**

The Principle Approach of American Christian Education
by Katherine Dang     **30**

Practicing American Christian Education—the Principle
Approach by James Rose     **39**

**Traditional Textbook Method**     **53**

The Traditional Schoolroom Approach: Bringing the
Classroom Home by Jenefer Igarashi and
Dr. Heather Allen     **56**

Homeschool Co-ops or How Not to Be an
Independent Ear by Jennifer Pepito     **68**

**Charlotte Mason Method**     **73**

The Charlotte Mason Method by Catherine Levison     **76**

**Unit Study Method**     **89**

Unit Studies by Jessica Hulcy     **92**

Unit Study Method by Jennifer Steward     **101**

**Special Needs Unit**                                   **113**
Special Needs by Christine M. Field                       **115**
Homeschooling Our Children with Special Needs
    by Sherry Bushnell                                    **141**

**Carschooling®**                                        **147**
Carschooling® Takes Homeschooling on the Road!
    by Diane Flynn Keith                                  **149**

**Eclectic Method**                                      **165**
Eclectic Homeschooling by Maggie S. Hogan with
    Tyler Hogan                                           **168**
The Importance of Seeing Ernest or The Adventure of
    Discovering the Design of God by Diana Waring         **177**

**Unschooling or Delight Directed Studies**              **189**
Delight Directed Studies by Dorothy Moore                **192**
The Moore Formula by Raymond Moore                        **203**
What Is Relaxed Homeschooling? by Mary Hood, Ph.D.        **222**

**Whole-Heart Learning**                                 **227**
The Dangers of Nonbooks by Dr. Ruth Beechick             **229**
The Power of Books and Reading by Sally Clarkson          **248**
Wholehearted Home Education by Clay Clarkson              **259**

*Each mind has its own method.*

—Ralph Waldo Emerson

# Acknowledgments

This book is a labor of love, designed for homeschooling parents everywhere, whether expectant, current, or veteran, with all author proceeds warmly dedicated to the special-needs homeschooling organization, National Challenged Home-schoolers Associated Network (NATHHAN).

The various authors throughout this book have each graciously given of their time, resources, and heart by devoting their author royalties to those working tirelessly at NATHHAN, a worthwhile, special group of people.

Melonie Murray, director of marketing and public relations at *The Old Schoolhouse (TOS) Magazine*, spent hours upon hours not only proofreading and writing detailed introductions to chapters but also gave far more of herself than what was expected. We are immensely grateful for her God-given skills, hard work, and care for the special-needs community. Anissa DeGrasse, an upbeat, natural leader who kept us well aware of looming deadlines, worked as our main liaison with the publishers and provided much-needed support to those working closely on the book. Special thanks to Debbie Doane who edited for hours upon end, worked with authors, and took care of initial logistics with this project. All three are wonderful friends not only to *TOS* and this project, but to us, Paul and Gena, as well.

Thank you to personal friends who have given of themselves and blessed us abundantly with encouragement, love, and undying support: Geoff and Jenefer Igarashi, Mark and Kate Kessler, Brian and Stacey Salmonson, Christine Field, Diana Waring, George and Chris Calhoun, John and Diane Wheeler, Mike and Carol Halpin, Scott and Jennifer Pepito, Richard and Deborah Wuehler, Nancy Baetz, Heather Allen and family, Marc and Lisa Barthuly, Mia Harper, John and Patricia Tirado, Jim and Kris Price, and Ralph Moore. Each of you is special, and we thank you for your love and friendship.

# Introduction

Homeschooling families have shared with us these all-too-frequent questions: How is *this* method employed? Where would one begin to discover *that* method? Various styles of homeschooling abound, from unit study to classical to Charlotte Mason to unschooling to the principle approach and so on. Perhaps you are considering a mixture of all of the above (eclectic). With approximately 2.5 million children receiving their education at home in this country, several specific methodologies of imparting knowledge have sprung up over the years. *Why?* One reason is that all children are created uniquely, and unlike a teacher conducting classes for a roomful of thirty children, parents instinctively know their children well. They know that their young ones are different from each other. Each learns at his or her own pace; each grasps concepts and learns needed skills in his or her own way. Some children learn better in groups; others fare well with independent studies. Some learn faster when they are using their hands or can be outside; others learn best in an accelerated, more rigid atmosphere.

There is no cookie-cutter method for teaching and learning, not in a homeschool anyway. Within these pages you will discover some of the main "subheadings," if you will, of education at home. You may have been homeschooling your children for a while now but are concerned because one of them is not

1

doing as well as you think he or she should be doing. Perhaps for this child a learning-style change could make the difference between forced, stagnant learning and a more exciting, whole education. The experts who follow are here to share how their specific learning model can work for your family—or maybe not your family but your neighbor's family. Or perhaps not your neighbor's *entire* family but one of their children.

Again, learning is individualized, and the key to making education successful is finding the most suitable method of learning for your child and then employing it. Our hope is that you will connect with one of the styles presented in this book for one or more of your children. God bless you as you seek to serve him, who has called you to a marvelous work in training up your children in a way they should go.

—Paul and Gena Suarez, Publishers
*The Old Schoolhouse Magazine*, LLC

# Classical
# Education Method

*Let him that is taught in the word communicate unto him that teacheth in all good things.*

—GALATIANS 6:6

✳  ✳  ✳

*Literature has a great natural power. Through it, we receive the gifted communication of other persons. In literature, perhaps more than through any other art form, we are able to get into the other man's shoes.*

—SUSAN SCHAEFFER MACAULAY

A classical, Christian education offers a focus on the great books of Western civilization, in-depth teaching of logic and critical thinking skills, and continued reference to classical languages such as Latin and Greek. The homeschool family using the classical model uses an approach based on the trivium, which correlates the curriculum to the phases of a child's cognitive development. During the elementary years (up to about age twelve), the student focuses on the memorization and recitation of facts and figures. The middle-school years encompass the logic stage as the child begins to acquire more independent and argumentative ways. The third phase, known as the rhetoric stage, covers the high school years and is the period during which the student takes the facts, analyzes them, and learns to share them eloquently.

Sometimes referred to as the "great books" method, this model teaches students about the history of the world through the great works of Western civilization. Originally begun in classical Greece and Rome, the trivium method was brought back to life by writer and educator Dorothy Sayers in *The Lost Tools of Learning*. As they progress through the various stages of development, classical students come to see the interconnectedness of all subjects based on the knowledge acquired through the curriculum. After gaining a good grasp of basic facts, the child learns how to analyze information and offer his point of view in a fluid and convincing manner. The Christian trained through the classical method learns the history of his faith and predominant culture, grasps the lessons for all mankind within that history, and can adequately answer the questions of others about his beliefs. For the family seeking an in-depth liberal arts style education, the classical Christian education covers the bases.

Classical education has grown swiftly with curriculum companies and books such as *The Well-Trained Mind* offering parents suggestions, support, and encouragement. Parents who desire to encourage independent thinking skills and pass on an ability to see the world through the light of the triumphs and trials of history are much impressed by classical education. In this section we will hear from two experts in the field who have chosen a classical Christian education for their families. Doug Wilson of

Canon Press and Christine Miller of Nothing New Press will share with us the basics of how to offer our children a classical education. Much as the students of Greece and Rome once learned from their teachers, we will walk through the stages of the trivium with these educators and come away with insight into an age-old instructional method that can offer us an in-depth home education.

# Classical and Christian Education

### *Douglas Wilson*

The great difficulty in providing your children with a classical and Christian education is similar to the difficulty that water has in running uphill. I have sought to encourage those engaged in this task with the observation that all of us are trying to provide an education that none of us received. And so the first difficulty in doing this is recognizing the impossibility of it. After that, everything is easy.

Of course, what is not possible with men is possible with God, and so we must begin this admittedly difficult task by trusting in him completely. The real issue is whether God has called us to it. If he has, then he will make a way. If he has not, then we would not please him by pursuing it, whether it was easy or difficult.

Jesus teaches us that students rarely surpass their teachers, and so this question of qualification enters right at the beginning. What it means when we are talking about classical and Christian education is that parents who undertake this form of education for their children, particularly in a homeschool setting, are resolving to be students as well as teachers. They may be just a little ahead of their students, learning things in order to teach them, but at some point they must acquire what they pass on. When our school made the decision (on principle) to teach Latin, we didn't have anyone around who knew Latin. But we made the decision anyway; I wound up going back to college to take Latin, and I learned enough to stay a jump or two ahead of my students.

The summary of this first principle is that in order to provide this kind of education for our children, we must be willing to work hard, and we must be willing for God to part the Red Sea from time to time. This really is a blood-sweat-and-tears endeavor.

But saying it is a difficult endeavor does not define the nature of the difficulty. What *is* classical and Christian education?

We will begin with the second part of the question first. What is Christian education? We have to begin by excluding one definition that is unfortunately common. Christian education should *not* be defined as any process of education undertaken by Christians. Because Christians have not been taken away to heaven as soon as they were converted and because we still live in a sinful, fallen world, it is still possible for us to sin. And we can sin in any arena where we function—spiritually, physically, or mentally. Christians can perform unchristian acts, and they can think unchristian thoughts. Among those unchristian thoughts might be thoughts on the nature and direction of education. Just as a Christian can (sinfully) shoplift something, so a Christian can (sinfully) think that history, math, and biology are neutral endeavors. But they are not.

Christian education occurs when the process of education for covenant children is being conducted in accordance with the requirements of Scripture. In other words, when children are being taught in the will of God, *that* is Christian education.

One of the fundamental requirements of Scripture in this regard is the requirement to recognize what theologians call the antithesis. At the beginning of human history, God placed hostility between the seed of the woman and the seed of the serpent. One of the first duties that we have in teaching our children (the seed of the woman) is the duty of teaching them to be wary of snakes. And this is a constant duty, everywhere necessary. Where I live in Idaho, on the Palouse, there are no rattlesnakes. But just thirty miles south of us, rattlesnake country starts. It would be foolish to walk around in the country down there without any regard for snakes. The Bible teaches us that the seed of the serpent can show up anywhere, and we have to beware. Spiritually speaking, there is no place to relax and say, "No snakes are possible here." And so we have to teach our children to beware.

Because education is the process of preparing them for life and all the assorted areas of life, we need to show how this antithesis is operative in every subject—language, history, science, math, and so on. In every subject men tell the truth about God, and in every subject they lie. It makes a difference who writes the history curriculum—Moses or Jeroboam. "These are the gods that brought us out of the land of Egypt" (see Exod. 32:4).

An active pursuit of the antithesis rests upon another fundamental assumption. Cornelius Van Til once said that the Bible is authoritative in everything it addresses, and it addresses everything. There is no neutral place where sinful men (or students) may go in order to absent themselves from what God is saying. God speaks always and everywhere. His Word does not speak directly on each subject. It is silent, for example, on software programming and how to take apart an internal combustion engine. The Bible is not an exhaustive encyclopedia. It is more like a key in the corner of a map that enables us to interpret everything on the map. There is no area of our lives where the authority of the Scriptures does not extend. This means that in Christian education, great emphasis will be placed on having the Scriptures function authoritatively in every aspect of that education. Of course this will not happen unless the people overseeing the education are Christians. But just having them be Christians does not guarantee it will happen. The Scriptures must be taken as the absolute bedrock.

This said, what does *classical* mean? This question can be divided in two, and we need to remember that it is not a *separate* question. If we say that the Christian aspect of this education is over here (authoritative over all), and the classical part is over there (not under authority), we have fallen into the old-fashioned trap of contradicting ourselves. Classical is not something that can be understood in isolation from Christ because *nothing* can be understood in isolation from Christ.

Under Christ *classical* refers to two things. The first has to do with the *content* of the education the students are receiving, principally in the areas of literature and history, but not absent in the other subjects. Classical education is commonly thought of as a "great books" program, and this is not far from the truth. To fill it out, we need to take a moment to determine what constitutes "great."

Most books that show up in great books curricula are part of what has been called the Western Canon. Those who complain about such books do so in favor of a broader and more eclectic multicultural offering and say that these books are too Western, too biased in the direction of Western civilization. But there is a reason for that bias, and it has nothing to do with any innate superiority of Europeans and their spawn around the globe.

The kingdom of God is not to be equated with Western culture, and Western culture does not constitute the fulfillment of "thy kingdom come." At the same time the history of the kingdom of God and the history of Western culture are so intertwined as to be incomprehensible apart from each other. Think of trying to explain Charlemagne without reference to the church or Augustine without reference to the late Roman Empire. In the providence of God, the gospel spread out from Palestine west and north, for the most part. Western civilization is not the kingdom of God, but it became great *because* of the kingdom of God. Consequently, the literature and history of all this is well worth the time it takes to learn and master, and it should be at the core of the education we provide our children. There is no need to be embarrassed about teaching our children their culture and their heritage. This is no disparagement to the culture of others. As I have said many times, it is not possible to teach children to honor other cultures by teaching them to despise their own. Children who are taught to honor their mother will know why other children honor *their* mothers.

But classical education also requires a particular pedagogical method, and this method has been called the trivium. *Trivium* is a Latin word referring to three-way intersection, and the three roads that run together here are grammar, dialectic, and rhetoric. In the formulation of some, dialectic is called logic. A generation ago the classical scholar and Christian writer Dorothy Sayers wrote an essay entitled "The Lost Tools of Learning." Her point was to take the medieval elements of the trivium and line them up with what she had observed about child development. She said in that essay that she was confident that no one was crazy enough to try what she was suggesting, but we decided to take her up on it anyway.

*Grammar* refers to the constituent elements of every subject. Grammar does not refer only to language; every subject has a grammar. Geography has rivers and mountains. Arithmetic has addition and subtraction tables. History has names and battles and dates. Each subject has a grammar. Sayers pointed out that children in the elementary years are going through what she called *the poll-parrot stage.* They love to chant, memorize, and recite. Since they love to do that anyway and will make up things to memorize if you don't give them things to memorize, why not cut with the grain? Why not have them take on grammar when that is what they love to do and that is what they are good at doing?

The next stage is the dialectic, which refers to the ordered relationships of all various bits of isolated data. In the grammar stage we have accumulated mounds of facts. In the dialectical stage we begin to sort them out and arrange them. This stage (roughly corresponding to the junior high years) is the time when the students have entered what Sayers called *the pert stage.* They have become somewhat argumentative. So then, she reasons, why not teach them to argue? When you teach formal symbolic logic to eighth graders, for some reason they eat it up. Again the point is to cut with the grain. At this stage students start learning more complicated math, grammatical relations in English and Latin, formal logic, and so on.

The stage corresponding with the rhetoric element of the trivium was called *the poetic stage* by Sayers. This occurs during the high school years, and it is the time when the students have become naturally concerned with keeping up appearances. Again we teach with the nature of the student, and we teach them the art of presenting themselves well—rhetoric. This stage is where they should take actual rhetoric courses along with an apologetics course and all their literature courses.

It can be admitted now that the first generation of classical and Christian educators did a good bit of flying by the seat of their pants. But fortunately for those who are just now beginning this exciting task, there are now piles upon piles of materials to help the classical and Christian homeschooler get started. We have sketched the grand theory, which is akin to looking at the wonderful picture of the tricycle on the cover of the box. But

now comes the time for assembly, and you might hear the
ominous tinkling of countless nuts and bolts inside the box.
But don't worry—there are clear and cogent directions inside
the box (and they are not in Japanese), and they are readily
available from organizations like the Association of Classical
Christian Schools (ACCS), Logos School, Canon Press, and
Veritas Press.

※   ※   ※

Douglas Wilson is the pastor of Christ Church in Moscow,
Idaho. He is a founding board member of Logos School, a senior
fellow of theology at New St. Andrews College, and he serves as
an instructor at Grayfriars Hall, a ministerial training program at
Christ Church. He helped to establish the Confederation of
Reformed Evangelicals (CRE), is the editor of *Credenda Agenda*,
and the author of numerous books on classical Christian education, the family, the church, and the reformed faith. After serving
in the U.S. Navy in the submarine service, he completed B.A. and
M.A. degrees in philosophy and a B.A. in classical studies from
the University of Idaho. Douglas and his wife Nancy have three
children and a number of grandchildren.

# What Is Classical Education?

*Christine Miller*

C lassical education returns to the time-honored educational theory of the past. Beginning in classical Greece and Rome, and continuing through the Puritan and Colonial eras of our nation, children who received an education received a classical one. Classical education produced Archimedes, St. Paul, Dante, Leonardo da Vinci, Galileo, Isaac Newton, Christopher Columbus, Shakespeare, and our own great George Washington, Thomas Jefferson, and John Adams.

These giants of their times are only the tip of the iceberg of the great philosophers, scientists, theologians, writers, and artists who lived and worked through the eighteenth century. They lived up to their potential, and each in his own way impacted the course of human history because his potential was unlocked in part by classical education, which prepared him to grapple with the problems of his day.

The core of classical education is the trivium, which simply put is a teaching model that seeks to tailor the curriculum subject matter to a child's cognitive development. The trivium

emphasizes *concrete* thinking and memorization of the facts of
the subject matter in grade school, *analytical* thinking and
increased understanding of the subject matter in middle school,
and *abstract* thinking and articulation of the subject matter in
high school.

Several subjects are unique to classical education, which
helps accomplish the goals of the trivium: grammar, the science
of language usage; logic, the science of right thinking; and rhetoric, the science of effective verbal and written expression.
Classical Christian education is further characterized by a rich
exposure to the history, art, and culture of Western civilization,
including its languages (Latin and Greek), its philosophy and literature (the great books of Western civilization and the Christian
tradition), and the development of a biblical worldview with
theology in its proper place as the queen of the sciences.

The progression of learning from facts to understanding
to expression—the stages of the trivium—give children the
tools to think for themselves and to be independent, lifelong
learners. Thus the primary goal of classical education: to equip
educated men and women with the ability to approach previ-
ously unknown subject matter, problems, or life situations;
and using the tools of learning that have been practiced and
refined and internalized in school, to grasp the subject or problem, analyze it according to the standard of truth, and understand and do something about it. Classical education therefore
trains children for success in any field, whether it is marriage
and family life, work dealing with society and individuals,
business, or arts and the humanities. Furthermore, classical education has proven its effectiveness in training for scientific
excellence, which depends on the arts of fact-finding, analyza-
tion, adherence to truth, and the problem-solving skills in which
classical education specializes. Secondarily, it works: children
taught by this method routinely exhibit academic proficiency.

## The Core of Classical Education

Historically classical education was implemented primarily by studying only the three core subjects of each of the trivium stages: grammar, logic, and rhetoric. Thus, Latin and Greek grammar only was studied in the elementary years; logic only, using *Euclid's Elements*, was studied in the middle school years; and rhetoric only, using *Aristotle's Rhetoric*, was studied in the high school years. A correlation can be made between the historic core of classical education: Latin, Euclid, and rhetoric, and the emphasis on the three Rs in American education: reading (grammar), writing (rhetoric), and 'rithmetic (logic, via *Euclid's Elements*).

But it is even more helpful to understand why the historical core of classical education was as it was. It is because classical education carries a distinct language imperative; it is a completely language-centered education. The study of grammar teaches a child the standard of language usage and the meaning it conveys in the culture. The study of logic, which *Euclid's Elements* taught, is the next rung in the ladder of language mastery. It teaches a child how language conveys truth or falsehood and how to think rightly in language, as all thought occurs in language. The study of rhetoric is the next rung in the ladder of language mastery. It teaches a child how to communicate effectively and eloquently what is now known to be true. The three subjects of the stages of the trivium can really be thought of as the three stages of language mastery. At the end of his K through twelve classical education, a child can truly understand without being subject to manipulation by advertisers or politicians, and be truly understood: able to convey the exact nuance of meaning he intends to convey.

A classical education "leads" a child "out of" (*educare* in Latin) immature speaking, writing, reading, and thinking, and gives him what Richard Mitchell called (in *Why Good Grammar?*) "the power of his mind."

Why is this language mastery so important? God is a God of his word. He has chosen to reveal himself to man by the Word. "The Word became flesh, and dwelt among us, . . . full of grace and truth" (John 1:14 NASB). The infallible and immutable revelation of God to man contained in God's Word is expressed in the medium of language. This is why classical education was brought to this country by the first settlers; it was so that every child could be proficient in language to use as a tool in order to read and understand the Bible. In those days every pastor was facile in Hebrew, Greek, and Latin (grammar), able to tell truth from falsehood in his doctrine (dialectic), and able to expound eloquently on the Scriptures (rhetoric).

Furthermore, the commission of every Christian is to witness to the truth. The ability to express truth effectively and eloquently, the goal of rhetoric, is not optional for believers. While truth can be expressed by those who have not had a classical education or who have not gained the mastery of language that this unique education provides, we ought still to want, for the Lord's sake, to take advantage of all that education affords to make the most of our potential.

However, the historic core of classical education does not provide a curriculum comprehensive enough to meet the requirements of most state homeschooling laws. A truly optimum classical education, then, ought to be like a three-legged stool. One leg is the mastery of language: English and Latin grammar, logic, and rhetoric. The second leg is the mastery of mathematics: arithmetic, the grammar of mathematics; algebra and geometry, the logic of mathematics; and higher math, the rhetoric of mathematics. The third leg is Christian and Western civilization, so that the culture may be transferred from one generation to the next, allowing it to endure and progress. If ever a generation failed to transfer Christian and Western culture to the next generation, that culture would cease to exist upon the parent generation's death. Western civilization, which is based upon and is an outgrowth of Christianity, includes history, literature, art, music, science, philosophy, law, government, and other related topics, all on their biblical foundations.

Out of all these subsets of Western civilization, history and literature are the most important. History, because (1) the plan of salvation and the work of God among men rests on a historical foundation; (2) God has commanded parents to instruct children in what has happened before; and (3) the study of history helps impart wisdom and judgment to those who engage in it—foolish choices and their consequences are played out on the historical stage so that foolishness need not be repeated.

Literature, because, as C. S. Lewis wrote, in "Christianity and Literature" in *Christian Reflections*, literature's purpose is not for the author to create something originating with himself, not to bring "into existence beauty or wisdom which did not exist before, but simply and solely . . . to embody in terms of his own art some reflection of eternal Beauty and Wisdom."[1] The truly great literature of Western civilization reveals beauty and wisdom reflective of the beauty and wisdom inherent in God's nature.

Therefore, in the elementary years, the core emphasis of classical education would be: English instruction in grammar and writing mechanics; Latin or Greek grammar; arithmetic; knowledge of the history of Western civilization; and lots of practice reading the best children's literature that Western civilization has produced, all taught from a biblical worldview.

In the middle school years, the core emphasis of classical education would be: English instruction in formal logic and writing the argumentative essay; Latin or Greek grammar and reading in Latin or Greek; algebra and geometry; analysis of the history of Western civilization; and beginning to read and discuss the great books of the Christian and Western tradition, all taught from a biblical worldview.

In the high school years, the core emphasis of classical education would be: English instruction in formal rhetoric, practiced in speech, debate, and in writing; Greek or Hebrew or modern languages such as French or German; higher mathematics; economics, law, and political science based on an understanding of the history of Western civilization; and continuing to read and discuss the great books of the Christian and Western tradition, all taught from a biblical worldview.

## Classical Education in the Elementary Years

### ENGLISH

Grammar study contains three components: *letters,* which combined form *words,* which combined form *sentences.* Phonics for reading and spelling teaches letters. Word forms, such as learning roots, suffixes, prefixes, changes in verb tense or making nouns plural, homonyms, and so on teaches words. Syntax study through sentence diagramming teaches sentences. Additionally, children should learn the mechanics of writing, including proper spelling and its rules, in the elementary years. It is unreasonable to expect children to write original compositions before learning the tools of writing and spelling. Therefore copying sentences and paragraphs in grades one through four provides lots of penmanship practice and familiarity with correct English grammar and spelling; and dictation leading to original compositions in grades five and six provides the transition to original compositions and the chance to practice and refine what has been learned.

- Grades 1–2: Phonics for reading and spelling; copying for penmanship

- Grades 3–4: Word forms such as making plurals, suffixes, etc.; spelling; copying for penmanship; writing mechanics
- Grades 5–6: Sentence diagramming; spelling; dictation and original compositions; writing mechanics

## LATIN

Children are language sponges, so when to begin the study of Latin or Greek is up to the parent. Children are able to learn other languages easily from early on, and curriculum is available to teach children Latin or Greek beginning in first grade. Learning Latin helps in understanding English grammar, increases vocabulary, and teaches precise thinking skills, so it is helpful to begin Latin in the elementary years, but children will not be damaged for life if Latin is put off to the middle school years when they can do more independent study.

## ARITHMETIC

Avoid the new approach which de-emphasizes memorizing math facts or tries to teach algebra concepts too soon. A good curriculum will use manipulatives to teach new concepts, emphasize facts memorization, and provide lots of practice for both mental and written arithmetic.

## WESTERN HISTORY

History does not have to be dry and boring. Children love to read interesting historical narratives to learn what, who, where, and when. In addition, supplement the historical narrative with exciting historical novels, biographies, and nonfiction; create maps and time lines; create wall-size collages to illustrate the most important events of the era; cook authentic recipes, make costumes and art projects in the style of the era. Don't be surprised if history goes from the most hated to the most loved subject when historical facts are taught this way.

- Grade 1: Old Testament and Egyptian history
- Grade 2: Greek and Roman history
- Grade 3: Medieval history
- Grade 4: Renaissance, Reformation, exploration history
- Grade 5: American history
- Grade 6: Modern European and twentieth-century history

WESTERN LITERATURE

Read the best children's literature that has been written in English. Why settle for the latest poorly written series when Peter Rabbit, Winnie the Pooh, *The Merry Adventures of Robin Hood*, The Chronicles of Narnia, *The Wind in the Willows*, *The Little House on the Prairie*, and *Tom Sawyer* are available, to name a few?

## Classical Education in the Middle School Years

ENGLISH

Logic, the science of how truth or falsehood is conveyed in language, is the next subset of English study once grammar has been mastered. Begin with formal (Aristotelian) logic and then proceed to advanced modern logic. Many good curricula exist for middle school students. Original composition becomes the focus of writing exercises, with the goal at the end of the middle school years being writing a grammatically correct, tight, well-reasoned essay.

- Grade 7: Beginning formal logic; writing grammatically correct, clear, and smooth sentences
- Grade 8: Intermediate formal logic; writing topically narrow, supported, and logically ordered paragraphs; writing the argumentative paragraph

- Grade 9: Advanced logic; writing the topically narrow, supported, and logically ordered essay; writing the argumentative essay

## LATIN AND GREEK

If Latin was not studied in the elementary years, begin it now. Many good curricula exist for beginning Latin students in the middle school years. Otherwise continue in the course of Latin study begun in the elementary years. The goal is facile translation and reading in Latin. Once Latin study has been completed, add Greek.

## MATHEMATICS

Once arithmetic has been mastered, go on to algebra. The whole study of algebra should be undertaken at one time; do not divide algebra I and II with a year of geometry. Algebra is the language in which all the higher mathematics discourse, including geometry. Once algebra has been mastered, then any higher math study can follow it in any order, but geometry with proofs is recommended next, as it builds on the foundation of logic begun in English. If your student needs more work in arithmetic, please provide it before moving on to algebra. If your student needs more work in algebra, please provide it before moving on to geometry. In classical education the criterion for going on to the next level of any subject is mastery, not keeping up with the schedule in the book. Children are individuals, and one reason we homeschool is to provide them with a curriculum tailored to them, not "one size fits all."

- Grade 7: Algebra I
- Grade 8: Algebra II
- Grade 9: Geometry

## WESTERN HISTORY

In the elementary years, students learned the who, what, when, and where of history. In the middle school years, students review Western history again, this time analyzing the events and choices made by the players and their outcomes and comparing them to the standard of truth—God's ways—as presented in the Bible. Students read the classic histories of Western civilization and discuss what they are learning with their teacher or other knowledgeable mentor. In the discussions it is important for the teacher to challenge the students to defend their statements logically and encourage them to look for fallacies in others' statements. The Western history study also provides topics for essays in English.

- Grade 7: Old Testament, Greek, and Roman history
- Grade 8: Medieval, Renaissance, Reformation, and exploration history
- Grade 9: American and modern history

## WESTERN LITERATURE

Continue reading the best novels and literature that have been written in English. In ninth grade, begin reading the great books of Western civilization. A student should expect to read about sixteen to twenty of the one hundred great books in the four years from ninth to twelfth grade to do them justice. Discuss the philosophies and worldviews presented in the literature and how the biblical worldview is supported or destroyed. In the discussions it is important for the teacher to challenge the students to defend their statements logically and encourage them to look for fallacies in others' statements.

## Classical Education in the High School Years

ENGLISH

Rhetoric, the science of effective and elegant communication, is the next subset of English study once logic has been mastered. The emphasis is on both oral and written communication. If debating clubs are available, your student would benefit greatly by becoming involved. In the final year of high school, the student should pass both a written essay and oral examination of comprehensive topics studied in his twelve years of education and demonstrate mastery of grammatically correct, logically sound, and elegantly effective written and oral communication.

- Grade 10: Principles of rhetoric; writing the effective paper; beginning speech and debate
- Grade 11: Principles of rhetoric; writing the research paper; debate
- Grade 12: Senior research paper; senior oration; debate

LATIN AND GREEK OR MODERN LANGUAGES

The student should continue his studies in Latin and/or Greek, or if completed, begin Hebrew or modern foreign languages such as Spanish or German, if desired.

MATHEMATICS

Students continue their math studies with the higher mathematics of trigonometry, elementary functions, and calculus. Since the highest math necessary to do well on the SAT or ACT is mastery of algebra and geometry, students may instead study the mathematics of music or visual design or the history of mathematical discovery, if desired.

## APPLIED WESTERN HISTORY

The studies of economics, law, and political science are direct outgrowths of Western civilization, and too often students enter their adult life after school with little knowledge of these important fields that exert great influence on our daily lives.

- Grade 10: Economics
- Grade 11: Law and the Constitution
- Grade 12: Political Science

## WESTERN LITERATURE

Continue reading the great books of Western civilization begun in the ninth grade. Discuss the philosophies and worldviews presented in the literature and how the biblical worldview is supported or destroyed. These discussions (as well as those from applied Western history) provide great topics for English papers and the senior research paper.

Classical education looks different from most public or private school education. American education has been systematically gutted for the past one hundred years, and classical education seeks to restore the high standards and effective outcomes (educated citizens) that were the hallmark of early American society. You might notice no emphasis on science, physical education, art, or other common "necessities" of modern education. These things and others can be added to the curriculum as each family and student determine is necessary, and information on the classical approach with curriculum suggestions for these additional subjects can be found on the author's Web site. However, the curriculum described above contains what is necessary to classical education, to meet most state standards, standardized test requirements, and SAT and ACT requirements. Specific curriculum suggestions and much more detailed information can be found on the author's Web site, www.classicalhomeschooling.org.

## Endnotes

1. C. S. Lewis, "Christianity and Literature" in *Christian Reflections* (Grand Rapids, MI: William B. Eerdmans Publishing Company, 1994).

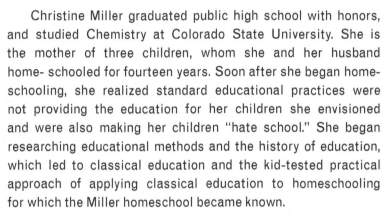

Christine Miller graduated public high school with honors, and studied Chemistry at Colorado State University. She is the mother of three children, whom she and her husband home- schooled for fourteen years. Soon after she began home-schooling, she realized standard educational practices were not providing the education for her children she envisioned and were also making her children "hate school." She began researching educational methods and the history of education, which led to classical education and the kid-tested practical approach of applying classical education to homeschooling for which the Miller homeschool became known.

She launched her family's homeschooling Web site, Classical Christian Homeschooling, in the spring of 1998 (www.classicalhomeschooling.org) and also began publishing curriculum materials for homeschoolers (www.nothingnew press.com). Her articles have appeared in *Homeschooling Today* as well as being reprinted in numerous local classical school and homeschool association newsletters and parent information manuals in the U.S. and overseas.

# Principle
# Approach Method

*These things command and teach. Let no man despise thy youth; but be thou an example of the believers, in word, in conversation, in charity, in spirit, in faith, in purity. Till I come, give attendance to reading, to exhortation, to doctrine.*

—1 TIMOTHY 4:11–13

❋   ❋   ❋

*There is one academic subject in which we need to go far, far beyond public school standards. We need to provide the best available instruction in the history and geography of our nation. While the public schools are drowning children in the academically meaningless and morally damaging world of "multiculturalism," we should be teaching our children to thoroughly know the history and philosophies of the men and women who founded this country. If*

*American children are not taught the principles of freedom, America will not be free for very long.*

—MICHAEL FARRIS

F or the Christian family attempting to sort out a philosophy of education, no method appears to be as biblically based or as utterly American as the principle approach. Speaking specifically of the divine hand of God in American history, the principle approach requires that both the student and the teacher examine all subjects using the teachings of the Bible. Students come to see the hand of God, or providence, throughout the curriculum. Through a renewal of the "4-R" method of learning, the student learns to examine all that is placed before him through a Christian worldview. Because the biblical principles are the basis of the entire method of education, it has been said that without God there is no "principle approach." If we embrace the idea that there is one God working through mankind to establish nations throughout history, we cannot then remove him from the history of those nations. Most specifically, the principle approach explains to us that the hand of God has guided the creation of the United States of America. Because it is established upon the Christian principle of self-government, America cannot be removed from the equation either.

Homeschool families using this method will research the facts of a topic, use their discernment to reason out information and to relate to it through their biblical worldview. Both student and teacher will record the steps involved in the process and the lessons learned. Throughout the entire process both parties are consciously aware of the hand of God in the subjects studied and constantly relate to the subject manner from that viewpoint. A specific text need not be purchased, nor does grade level matter so much as becoming able to govern oneself using biblical principles.

To explain in more depth the concepts of the principle approach and help us discover how best to implement it, we turn to Katherine Dang of Universal History and James Rose of the American Christian History Institute. As we learn from our experts, they will walk us through these steps in relation to learning literature and botany. They show us how to incorporate the four Rs into an overall method of educating the child rather than breaking them down into individual steps that focus on details while forgetting the principle (or "seed") of the matter. Should you feel the principle approach is the most appropriate path for your family, these educators offer the steps to begin the journey.

# The Principle Approach of American Christian Education

## Katherine Dang

H ow many American Christians have a philosophy of education? How many realize that every philosophy of education is predicated upon a philosophy of government? Or that
every philosophy of government has its own prescribed philosophy of education? One's philosophy of education is insepara-
ble from a philosophy of government. The content and method
in the education of a people result in their own peculiar form of
government. There are only two forms of government: atheistic
and Christian.

## Atheism's Form of Government

Atheism, the religion of unbelief, asserts, "There is no God,"
and therefore no necessary regard for the spiritual life of the
individual. According to the atheist, the "evolved" or educated
human being puts away any idea or hope of life beyond the

material world of the senses. It is "nonprogressive" to live conscientiously before a God and a "superstition" that is a psychological aberration and an impediment to one's progress in society and in the real world. It is better to live pragmatically about our material existence and survival, for all we have is this life and this lifetime.

Unbelief has its own system of education, and the content of this system of education evolves or morphs from one kind of curriculum into another. Each of these curricula, however, is still the same human wisdom pitted against the wisdom of God.

Is it not true that, in the mind of the atheist, the highest power and achievement of social order lies within the state, where all power is centralized for the managing of *all* the concerns of collective society? Reasoning from atheism's view that the source of all authority and power is in the centralized state, it follows that the more centralization there is in society, the greater the good for everyone in society.

Human wisdom says that one's well-being is entirely dependent on the well-being of the collective. Men must live harmoniously, collectively together with others if anyone is to survive at all. All men have is one another; they therefore must learn or be conditioned to sacrifice their self-interests for the interests of the collective and to tolerate differences of opinion, customs, and ways of thinking and living. Men must learn to be socially accountable and accepting of one another. This learning to be socially accountable and accepting is a conditioning process of acquiring a social conscience in order that no one part of society offends another. The socially conscientious base their decisions upon what others might think or do, upon what public opinion and the will of the majority or popular will are, each of which necessarily evolves, or changes, from age to age, from fashion to fashion.

Collective harmony, social acceptance, and social conscientiousness are achieved by social equalization through one common, universal, standardized educational system, controlled and regulated by the broadest centralization.

## Christianity's Form of Government

The Scriptures are clear: "God is" (Heb. 11:16); "man does not live by bread alone" (Deut. 8:3 NASB and Matt. 4:4 NASB); "every one of us shall give account of himself to God" (Rom. 14:12); and in God there "is no variableness, neither shadow of turning" (James 1:17).

The biblical alternative to atheistic education is an educational system that aims at equipping the individual to be accountable to his Maker and to be independently dependent on God, who is the supreme judge of the world.

The absolute power of God is the highest of all powers and wisdom. In the sight of a just God, all men have equal worth. All men are equal under his law. Each man has from God his own personal life, liberty, and property, for which each individual must give him account, whereby "to whom much is given, much is required."

God does not coerce or manipulate man's obedience to him. According to his law of reason, God reveals and teaches man his will and purposes and would have, then, voluntary obedience from whomever should conclude that obedience to God is the most reasonable thing.

Deuteronomy 6:6 indicates: (1) that biblical education in the home begins when the parents own—internalize for themselves—the laws of God pertaining to the education of children, and (2) that, in making their decisions regarding the education of their children, parents be governed by the spirit and intent of God's—not man's—laws of education. If, in the education of children, the Scriptures are simply "attached" to subject matter and there is a failure of instructing children in the underlying, supporting principles of ideas and facts, the point of true, scriptural education is lost.

Having children hide the Word of God in their hearts involves so much more than their rote memorization of Scripture, but it is also their making the Word of God central or the seat of their *individual government* in all the affairs of daily life and living, making the principles of God's Word the individual's rule of life. Children are to grow in their understanding of the principles of the subjects they are taught and, then, to be exercised in their own individual reasoning in, by, and with those principles.

As a method, the "principle approach," per se, is really only one of the three constituents—aim, content, and method—of a broader idea: the philosophy of American Christian education, the biblical alternative to the philosophy of progressive education.

## Contrasting Aims

Modern, progressive education is the educational philosophy of *socialism*. Socialism prescribes an education that aims to instill those spiritual, moral, and mental qualities of individual character that are most conducive to an individual's dependency on an all-powerful state: infidelity, irresponsibility, and ignorance.

As individual self-government is the cornerstone of America's constitutional federal republic, American Christian education aims to instruct and discipline individuals in accordance with the principles of character and conscience that are fundamental and supportive of *individual self-government*. Individual, personal faith in the absolute power of God in every area of life and living is indispensable to the continued life and existence of a Christian republic, which America is. America is a Christian republic because the cornerstone of America's form of government is Christianity's form of government—individual self-government in which a man's reason is governed by God and is obedient to him. When Christianity declines in the life of the individual American Christian, America will decline into socialism and, thus, become like all other nations of the world.

## Contrasting Content

While progressive education constructs an educational system on the idea that man is most importantly a social being, its educators will rely upon a state-enforced, uniform curriculum to advance social equality. The content and methodology of education are made uniform for the sake of outward equality, or standardization, by state mandate. The process of standardization in education, therefore, collectivizes subjects. This is an education not in principles but rather in conformity to socialization.

In the collectivization of subjects (e.g., language arts for grammar, literature, and composition; life sciences for botany, zoology, physiology, and anatomy; earth sciences for astronomy, geology, oceanography, physics, and chemistry; and social studies for geography, history, and government), mastery of the principles of a subject is a secondary aim to instruction. In order to fulfill the true aims of progressive education, it is far more important that students experience subjects in a social setting than that individual students in the collective society of the school or "class" comprehend the subjects themselves. It is far more important for the individual to make "social progress" than for him to advance in his individual scholarship.

For the individual scholarship demands a mastery of principles, which necessarily refer to his being fixed in absolute law. In socialization, however, there is no room for principle, when the aim of socialism is to establish the popular and collective will as the supreme authority in every area of the individual's life and living. American Christian education requires that each individual student be taught the biblical origin, content, purpose, and principles of each of his subjects. God, who created the universe and all that is therein, has established his perfect laws for everything he creates. Man's earthly progress and happiness depend on his trust in these laws, God's laws. It therefore behooves man to know and be knowledgeable of all of God's laws, both moral and physical. Such laws are discernible only as subjects are taught according to their God-given individuality: origin, content, purpose, and rudiments or first principles.

Parents and teachers have no obligation beyond establishing in their students the rudiments, that which is to be first learned or the seed, of each of his subjects: the biblical origin and content, biblical purpose and principles.

At a time in America when most of the available textbooks are secular in content, when biblical scholarship is weak, when self-teaching texts are no longer in mode, it has become necessary for the American Christian, independently and alone, to restore to himself a knowledge of the rudiments of all sorts of subjects through 4-R-ing: researching, reasoning, relating, and recording. One, however, does not "4-R" till he or she "drops" (from exhaustion). With *Webster's* 1828 and Bible in hand, once one has ascertained the above-mentioned biblical origin, content, purpose, and rudiments of a subject, one may *stop*. The four Rs approach is simply a practical means by which one is able to internalize knowledge, to take individual possession of it, rather than to follow after the traditions of men or imitate or copycat someone else's thoughts and ideas. The teacher is, instead, the source and origin of whatever he teaches. The desirable end result is to ascertain what must be laid down as foundations within each individual before he is prepared for self-teaching and self-advancement in any given subject. (See examples from botany and literature.)

## Contrasting Methods or Approaches

Progressive education approaches a student as if he were a product of evolution, a higher order of animal, denying him his spiritual aspect, his soul. Progressive education, therefore, is ultimately politically oriented if man cannot attain any existence higher than that of belonging to the state or world community. Children are necessarily socialized at the expense of spiritual and intellectual development. They are subjected to every available kind of collective activity and experience: grouped projects, conditioned learning through programmed stimuli, sensory experiences, and nonreflective exercises—all of which weaken the individual's capacity for independent action. Gradually, over time, this method establishes his dependency upon consensus judgments made through democratic decision-making processes. And if, in the process, individual property of conscience is violated, little or no matter is made of it. To achieve its political ends, progressive education need only appeal to the base instincts of man: his animal appetites and human passions.

The Scriptures approach man as a rational creation of God, his rational part being the human soul. American Christian education would appeal to the higher and nobler aspects of man, those aspects being his reason and his conscience. If a man acts in accord with a conscience enlightened and guided by the Word of God, he cannot offend God or man. An education from the Bible is an education of the conscience. If a man's appetites and passions be subject to his reason, and his reason be governed by God and obedient to him, he is self-governed. The art of self-government is the art of biblical reasoning: the ability to

reason from fixed, absolute principles—of every subject taught—
to satisfactory conclusions and conscientious applications.

We may either follow the coursework and systems of
unbelief, or we may follow the Scriptures, which teach that the
approach to teaching children is "here a little" and "there a little."
Scriptural education is an education in those principles that God
himself established for the universe he created.

Home educators have the opportunity, under God, to restore
self-government and self-education to themselves. United in
American Christian education, American Christian families may
individualize or customize their home education according to
the dictates of their Christian conscience. Does the American
Christian parent believe that what God has for his child could be
anything else but superior to what unbelief has to offer?

Parents and teachers of the twenty-first century have known
no other philosophy of education than that of progressive education. We have known no other approach to education but a secular one. But given to this generation is the work of building anew,
to the glory of God, the education in the Bible that shall lead this
and other nations into greater expressions of individual self-government. In the twenty-first century, the classic work of American
Christian education is *A Guide to American Christian Education
for the Home and School—the Principle Approach* by James B. Rose,
president of the American Christian History Institute. Patiently
begin.

✻   ✻   ✻

Katherine Dang is teacher and author, a Chinese American
Christian, native to the San Francisco Bay Area, and involved in
American Christian education for over thirty-five years. She has

taught and developed the rudiments and curriculum guides for a variety of subjects including physical geography, universal history, American history, literature, science, grammar, government, and economics for both elementary and secondary levels. For sixteen years, Katherine Dang was the administrator of a school that she helped found for grades kindergarten through senior high school. She is currently the founder and president of Philomath Foundation, a nonprofit, religious foundation established to propagate the ideas of providential history, self-government, and American Christian education.

Besides speaking at conferences, her activities involve the conducting of American Christian education seminars, youth courses, history and government study groups for adults, and teacher training courses. She is the author and editor of the published works: *Universal History, Volume I: Ancient History—Law without Liberty* and *Universal History, Volume II: Middle History—the Law of Liberty.*

# Practicing American Christian Education— the Principle Approach

## James Rose

To PRACTICE: performance; distinguished from theory; to use or exercise for instruction or discipline.[1]

American Christian education is the primary purpose or objective of the principle approach. The principle approach is secondary. It is a method of biblical reasoning that is *of* or *proceeding from* American Christian education, which is a philosophy of education that emphasizes the providence of God in history and the biblical principles of self and civil government. This approach to teaching and learning presupposes (1) that *every* philosophy of education is based on a *philosophy of history and government,* i.e., upon one's view of who or what is the source of authority and direction to teach and learn; and (2) that every form and function of civil government is an effect of a philosophy of education.

This article purposes to explain how to use or exercise the principle approach of American Christian education in the home and school. It is recommended that the thoughtful reader consider performing the instructions and illustrations suggested in this article in conjunction with the companion discourse on the principle approach by Katherine Dang.

American Christian education embraces a philosophy or view of history and government: the view that there is only one God (Providence) working through men and nations *in history*, and only one God governing internally (manifested as individual self-government), and that the wonderful works and government of God are revealed externally through three divine institutions—the local self-governing *family* and *church* and in *civil government*.

American Christian education teaches America's Christian history and government. Now let's be perfectly candid: a knowledge of American Christian *history* (God working in America to advance individual liberty) and *government* (the biblical principles of civil and self-government) benefits every American, not just the Christian, no matter his race, nationality, color, or religion. American Christian education does not deify America or Americans. It acknowledges God as providence and teaches that what is *good* in America—the great expression of individual liberty and self-government expressed in our history—*is God working in America*. This philosophy of education equips the Christian to relate Christ and Christianity to the character and conduct of his nation. In what nation during the history of civilization has the individual enjoyed the *greatest expression* of individual liberty, self-government, private property, and voluntary association under a constitutional form of civil government? Although *every* nation has a providential history, meaning there is evidence of the providence or *hand of God* (his eternal purpose and executive power) working in each nation, America has a *uniquely Christian origin* because it is established upon the Christian principle of self-government.

As Miss Dang explains in the accompanying article, as individual self-government is the cornerstone of America's constitutional federal republic, *American Christian education aims to give instruction and discipline individuals in accordance to the principles of character and conscience that are fundamental and supportive to individual self-government.*

Historically, the phrase *principle approach* denotes two applications, a general and a specific use. The general application of the phrase *principle approach* is to describe the seven minimal biblical principles that explain the relationship between God, Christian character, and conscience, and how to draw near and comprehend the biblical ground and foundation of America's Christian history and government. The specific application of the phrase *principle approach* is to America's historic Christian method of biblical reasoning and how one discovers and practically teaches the truths of God's Word through subjects in the curriculum. This article addresses how one may practice biblical reasoning through the four Rs to discover and develop the rudiments of a subject.

The principle approach is America's historic Christian *method of biblical reasoning,* which *makes the truths of God's Word the basis of every subject in the school curriculum.* The principle approach begins (*but does not end*) by restoring the four Rs to teaching and learning: researching, reasoning, relating, recording.[2] The goal or objective of American Christian education is *individual self-government.* The method to achieve this goal is *biblical reasoning,* America's historic Christian method of biblical reasoning using the four Rs to deduce the content, biblical origin, purpose and first principles or rudiments of each subject in the school curriculum.

## Fulfilling the Biblical Standards for American Christian Education

I recommend this approach to teaching and learning because it fulfills the following biblical standards for American Christian education:

1. Let (allow; to give power by a positive act) the teacher be conscious of the light of God's Word and make it appear to the student in each subject of the curriculum.
2. Let the teacher know there is only one God working and teach God's providence to the student through each subject.
3. Let self-government and biblical reasoning be cultivated in the teacher and student through the content and methods of education.
4. Let the first principles and ideas of the subject—its rudiments (not all the facts about it)—appear to the teacher and student as clearly identified and named.
5. Let the growth of Christian character and conscience develop gradually in the teacher and the student as one teaches a subject.

This approach or manner of instruction enables one to bring both the subject and the student into obedience to Christ and Christian principles. It equips one to use a wider variety of resources and not have to be dependent upon one textbook. It focuses on the spirit of a subject (the biblical origin and purpose or reason for teaching it) and not just simply knowing the facts or letter of a discipline, as important as the facts are. I esteem an approach that enables me to know God and make him known, thus enabling both the student and me to draw near and take possession of Bible truths through the four Rs.

## Expounding the Four Rs and Their Biblical Basis

Understand that the four Rs are *not steps* or gradations of biblical reasoning. One does not first research, then independently reason and subsequently relate then record. The mind does not work that way. No, the four Rs are done *simultaneously*, holistically, as a pastor would prepare a sermon or a teacher an original lesson by consciously searching for truth and, *at the same time*, reasoning to some conclusions, expounding or explaining ideas to himself, and writing down his conclusions.

Presupposing truth is *revealed* in God's Word, and one knows how to *read*, one *researches* or seeks diligently to identify the first principles that govern the subject. *At the same time* one *reasons* or deduces inferences from the principles or premises discovered. As one reflects upon the principle or truth of a subject, he *relates* (the biblical term is *to expound)* the subject to himself and the student by explaining and making clear to the understanding the connection between the principle(s) and the student's character, conscience, and his stewardship of the subject. As this mental and spiritual work is in progress, one *records* or writes down what is to be remembered, which means both the teacher and the student ought to make a written record of their application of biblical principles and purposes to the subject and to themselves in the four Rs. The four Rs require biblical reasoning and develop self-government.

The biblical basis for the four Rs is explicit. *Researching*, or searching again, is demonstrated by the apostles and disciples in John 5:39; Acts 17:11; and 1 Peter 1:10. *Reasoning* is illustrated in 1 Samuel 1:18; Acts 17:2; and 1 Peter 3:15. *Relating* or expounding is practiced in Acts 18:26 and clearly demonstrated by the Lord Jesus in Luke 26:27. *Recording* is manifested in Habakkuk 2:2; Luke 1:1–4; 1 John 5:10; and Revelation 1:1–3.

Remember the purpose of 4 R-ing a subject: it is to deduce the *rudiments* of a subject, the principles or first things to be learned. The rudiments of a subject are, metaphorically, the seed of any academic discipline from which anything springs; first principle; original.[3] We render the seed or rudiments of a subject as consisting of four constituents: its *content, origin, purpose, and principles*. The *whole* subject is comprehended in its seed—these four constituents or rudiments—and composes the foundation for developing the details of the curriculum and choosing textbooks or resources to teach, illustrate, and demonstrate the seed of a subject.

## How to 4 R a Subject

Understanding that the four Rs are exercised simultaneously, there is a *path* of reasoning, which involves ordered steps to deducing the rudiments of every subject, that is, its content and its biblical source, purposes, and principles.

Miss Katherine Dang has prepared two examples of the result of 4 R-ing literature and botany, illustrations which I shall use to explain how to use America's historic method of biblical reasoning to comprehend the whole subject in seed form.

Begin by *defining* (explaining the thoughts and significance which a word is understood to express) a subject in *Webster's 1828 American Dictionary of the English Language*. Noah Webster's dictionary is preferred for this step because of the clarity and precision of meaning embraced in his definitions.

Furthermore, as Miss Rosalie Slater reasoned, *Webster's 1828 American Dictionary* remains today the pure repository of three essential ingredients of America's Christian history. It reflects our Christian philosophy of life, our Christian philosophy of government, and our Christian philosophy of education. Unmistakably it reveals the degree to which the Bible was America's basic textbook and how it was related to all fields. Noah Webster as a Christian scholar, laid his foundation of etymology upon the Scriptures and his research into the origin of language stems from this premise. One cannot read his definitions or study his discussion of the grammatical construction of our language without encountering at every point a scriptural Christian philosophy of life.[4]

### EXAMPLE: 4 R-ING LITERATURE

As the example of 4 R-ing *literature* suggests on page 48, write out the definition of *literature* and underline the key words Webster uses to explain the distinctive *properties* (the peculiar qualities inherent or naturally essential to the discipline) of the subject you wish to comprehend. In this illustration, the key words are in **bold print,** i.e., **learning; acquaintance** with **letters or books; knowledge.** Continue defining key words in Webster's dictionary until the seed, the essential properties of the subject, are ascertained.

For example, **learning** is the knowledge of principles or facts received by instruction or study, and **knowledge** is determined by a clear and certain perception of that which exists, or of truth and fact; we can have no knowledge of that which does not exist. God has a perfect knowledge of all his works. If one needs to comprehend more of the significance of the key words in subsequent definitions, look them up, write them out, and *reason* from what you have read to deduce the seed, the ground or foundation, from which *learning* from books spring.

As step two, with the aid of a Bible concordance, begin searching the Bible for the vocabulary of literature and begin to *think* and ask questions of yourself: What does the Bible say about letters or books that will acquaint us with learning and knowledge? What is the source and origin of knowledge according to God's Word? For what purpose did God write? What are the first things/thoughts we ought to know and learn when we teach literature?

From 4 R-ing literature, we discern that the Bible is literature, written for our learning that we might have hope (Rom. 15:4). Philippians 4:8 outlines the standard, the rule or measure by which literature is to be judged as godly or ungodly. And 1 Corinthians 10:11 suggests that literature that meets God's standards is written for our admonition for reproof of a fault.

Following this preliminary search of the Bible concerning literature, there are three columns of possible conclusions to the following questions: In column one, the biblical origin of literature answers the questions, Are conclusions regarding who or what in the Bible is the source and origin of real, worthy knowledge (learning or literature)? Column two, the biblical purpose of literature, answers the question, What are God's purposes for knowledge (principles or facts) and learning (perception of the truth)? Column three suggests at least five biblical principles (ground or foundation) for building a course of study, a curriculum, in the literature of any subject: hearing, searching, teaching, instruction, and study.

The biblical principles of literature suggested in column three were deduced by asking the question, What is the ground or support for acquiring learning, an acquaintance with letters or books, or knowledge? Reasoning biblically, one may deduce that hearing increases learning; that God not only searches us, but we are instructed to research the *best* literature, the Scriptures (John 5:39; Acts 17:11; 1 Peter 1:10), and reason from them; that the Spirit of the Lord is the primary teacher of truth; that knowledge walks with a love of instruction; and that individual, independent study is approved of God.

# BOTANY

(Webster's 1828)

That branch of natural history which treats of **vegetables**; a science which treats of the different **plants**, and of the **distinguishing marks** by which each **individual species** may be known from every other.

Or, botany is the science of the **structure, functions, properties, habits and arrangements** of plants, and of the **technical characters** by which they are distinguished.

| Content | Origin | Principles |
|---|---|---|
| • Vegetables, plants<br>• Distinguishing marks of individual species<br>   • Structure, functions, properties, habits, arrangements, technical characters of | And God said, Let the earth bring forth grass, the herb yielding seed, and the fruit tree yielding fruit after its kind, whose seed is in itself, upon the earth: and it was so.<br>Genesis 1:11 | For the invisible things of him from the creation of the world are clearly seen, being understood by the things that are made, even his eternal power and Godhead, so that they are without excuse. . . .Rom 1:20 |

**Vegetable**

A plant; an organized body destitute of sense and voluntary motion, deriving its nourishment through pores or vessels on its outer surface, in most instances adhering to some other body, as the earth, and in general, propagating itself by **seeds**. Some vegetables have spontaneous motion, as the sunflower. Vegetables alone have the power of deriving nourishment from inorganic matter, or organic matter entirely decomposed. Gen. 1:11-12, 29, 2:5, 8-9

**Plant**

A vegetable; an organic body, destitute of sense and spontaneous motion, adhering to another body in such a manner as to draw from it its nourishment, and having the power of propagating itself by seeds; "whose seed is in itself." This definition may not be perfectly correct, as it respects all plants, for some **marine plants** grow without being attached to any fixed body.

The woody or **dicotyledonous** plants consist of three parts; the bark or exterior coat, which covers the wood; the wood which is hard and constitutes the principal part; and the pith or center of the stem. In **monocotyledonous** plants the ligneous or fibrous parts, and the pithy or **parenchymatous**, are equally distributed through the whole internal substance; and in the **lower plants**, funguses, sea weed, &c. the substance is altogether parenchymatous. By means of proper vessels, the nourishing juices are distributed to every part of the plant. In its most general sense, plant comprehends all **vegetables, trees, shrubs, herbs, grasses, &c.**

**Seed**

The substance, animal or vegetable, which nature prepares **for the reproduction and conservation of the species**. The seeds of plants are a deciduous part, containing the rudiments of a new vegetable. In some cases the seeds constitute the **fruit** or valuable part of plants, as in the case of wheat and other esculent **grain**; sometimes the seeds are inclosed in the fruit, as in apples and melons.

**Tree**

The general name of the largest of the vegetable kind, consisting of a firm woody stem springing from woody roots, and spreading above into branches which terminate in leaves. A tree differs from a shrub principally in size, many species of trees growing to the highth of fifty or sixty feet, and some species to seventy or eighty, and a few, particularly the pine, to a much greater highth, as nuciferous, or nut-bearing trees; baciferous, or berry-bearing; coniferous, or cone-bearing, &c. Some are forest-trees, and useful for timber or fuel; others are fruit-trees, and cultivated in **gardens and orchards**; others are used chiefly for shade and ornament. Gen.6:14

**Purpose**

And the Lord God took the man, and put him into the garden of Eden to **dress** it and to keep it. Gen. 2:15; Deut. 28:39

**Dress**

To adjust; to put in good order. Sometimes to till or cultivate. Gen. 4:2

**Keep**

To tend; to have the care of.

**Genesis 1:29**

And God said, Behold, I have given you every herb bearing seed, which is upon the face of all the earth, and every tree, in which is the fruit of a tree yielding seed; to you it shall be for meat. Deut. 8:8

**Genesis 2:16, 17**

And the Lord God commanded the man, saying, Of every tree of the garden thou **mayest freely eat**; But of the tree of the knowledge of good and evil . . . Gen. 42:2; Matt. 12:1; Mk. 2:23; Lk. 6:1-5

**Psalm 104:14**

He causeth the grass to grow for the cattle, and the herb **for the service of man**, that he may bring forth food out of the earth.

**Genesis 6:14**

Make thee an **ark of gopher wood** . . . II Chron. 9:21; Mk. 3:9, 4:37, 5:1, 2; Lk. 5:3; John 21:6, 8; Acts 20:13, 27:37, 28:11

**Deuteronomy 8:12**

. . . hast **built goodly houses**. . .

**Genesis 9:20**

And Noah began to be a husbandman; and he planted a **vineyard**.

**Revelations 22:2**

. . . and the leaves of the tree were for the **healing** of the nations.

**Leviticus 6:10**

The priest shall put on his linen **garment**. . . Prov. 31:24; Mk. 15:46; Lk. 23:53; John 19:40

**Jonah 4:6**

And the Lord God prepared a gourd, and made it to come up over Jonah, that it might be a **shadow over his head**, to deliver him from his grief. So Jonah was exceedingly glad of the gourd.

**Order:**

"organized"

**Magnitude:**

"largest of the vegetable kind,"

**Power:**

"whose seed is in itself," propagating itself by seeds.

"the power of deriving nourishment from inorganic matter, or organic matter entirely decomposed"

**Infinite Variety:**

"all vegetables, trees, shrubs, herbs, grasses, &c"

" trees are of various kinds"

**Beauty:**

"gardens and orchards"

"ornament"

©Katherine Dang

# LITERATURE

**Learning; acquaintance** with **letters or books**. Literature comprehends a **knowledge** of the ancient languages, denominated classical, history, grammar, rhetoric, logic, geography, &c. as well as of the sciences. A **knowledge** of the world and good breeding gives luster to literature.    —*Webster's 1828*

### Romans 15:4
For whatever things were **written** aforetime were **written for our learning**, that we, through patience and comfort of the scriptures, might have hope.

### Philippians 4:8
Finally, brethren, whatever things are **true**, whatever things are **honest**, whatever things are **just**, whatever things are **pure**, whatever things are **lovely**, whatever things are **of good report**; if there be any **virtue**, and if there be any **praise**, think on these things.

### I Corinthians 10:11
Now all these things happened unto them for ensamples, and they are **written for our admonition**, upon whom the ends of the world are come.

| Biblical Origin | Biblical Purpose | Biblical Principles |
|---|---|---|
| Isaiah 40:13–14<br>    Who hath directed **the Spirit of the Lord**, or being his counselor, hath taught him?<br>    With whom took he counsel, and who instructed him, and taught him in the path of judgment, and taught him knowledge, and showed to him the way of understanding?<br>Psalm 94:10<br>    He who chastiseth the heathen, shall not he correct: **He who teacheth man knowledge**, shall not he know?<br><br>II Chronicles 1:10, 11, 12<br>    **Give me, now, wisdom and knowledge**, that I may go out and come in before this people; for who can judge this, thy people, who are so great? . . . knowledge . . . that thou mayest judge my people, over whom I have made thee king, **Wisdom and knowledge are granted unto thee**. . . .<br><br>Daniel 1:17<br>    As for these four children, **God gave them knowledge and skill** in all learning and wisdom; and Daniel had understanding in all visions and dreams. | Acts 24:22<br>    And when Felix heard these things, having **more perfect knowledge of that way**, he deferred them,. . .<br>I Corinthians 15:34<br>    . . . Some have not **the knowledge of God**. I speak this to your shame.<br>Proverbs 9:10<br>    . . . the **knowledge of the holy** is understanding.<br>Proverbs 30:2–3<br>    Surely I am more brutish than any man, and have not the understanding of a man. I neither learned wisdom, nor have the **knowledge of the Holy One**.<br>Philippians 3:8<br>    . . . I count all things but loss **for the excellency of the knowledge of Christ Jesus**, my Lord;<br>I Timothy 2:4<br>    Who will have all men to be saved, and **to come unto the knowledge of the truth.**<br>II Timothy 3:7<br>    . . . to come to the knowledge of the truth.<br>Proverbs 24:5<br>    . . . yea, a man of knowledge **increaseth strength.**<br>Hosea 4:6<br>    My people are **destroyed for lack of knowledge**; because thou hast rejected knowledge. . . | Hearing<br>    A wise man will **hear**, and will increase learning. . . . Proverbs 1:5<br><br>Searching<br>    O Lord, thou hast **searched** me and known me. Psalm 139:1<br><br>Teaching<br>    Who hath directed the Spirit of the Lord, or being his counselor, hath **taught** him? With whom took he counsel, and who **instructed** him, and **taught** him in the path of judgment, and taught him knowledge, and **showed** to him the way of understanding? Isaiah 40:13–14<br><br>    And many people shall go and say, Come ye, and let us go up to the mountain of **the Lord**, to the house of the God of Jacob;and he **will teach us of his ways**, and we will walk in his paths. . . . Isaiah 2:3<br><br>Instruction<br>    Whoso loveth **instruction** loveth **knowledge**, but he that hateth reproof is brutish. Proverbs 12:1<br><br>Study<br>    **Study** to show thyself approved unto God, a workman that needeth not to be ashamed, rightly dividing the word of truth. II Timothy 2:15 |

## Example: 4 R-ing Botany

Page 47 is an example of what one may deduce by 4 R-ing botany. The format or form of how the rudiments of this subject are rendered is slightly different, but all the constituents are identified. First, *Webster's 1828 American Dictionary* is used to define the essential parts of botany.

Column one summarizes the basic content of a course in botany, which is comprised of four constituents: vegetables, plants, seeds, and trees. Column two combines two essential elements: (1) the biblical origin of botany, that is, on the third day, God created all the elements of botany, and (2) among the biblical purposes for studying botany are to dress (put in good order) and keep (care for) the plants God provides for us to eat, to build useful tools and shelter, to use for healing or curative therapy, and to make clothing and coverings.

In column three, Romans 1:20 suggests that the eternal mind and power of God are the foundation for five principles for comprehending the subject. The study of plants reveals and reflects God's (1) orderliness, (2) magnitude (large and small plants), (3) power (to reproduce and nourish), (4) infinite variety and individuality (differences in the same or other species of plants), and (5) the great beauty and comeliness of plants. These five terms also reveal the attributes of God as reflected in his creation of plants or flora. A careful reading of the definitions in column one will confirm the vocabulary of these five principles.

To review, *Webster's* definitions of a subject reveal the essential vocabulary and properties that constitute the *content* of the discipline. From the vocabulary of the subject one 4 Rs the Scriptures—the whole counsel of God—for the biblical *origin*, *purpose*, and *principles*, the seed or rudiments of the entire subject. From this biblical and academic foundation, one begins to build a course of study and to discern the scholarship of others in the field that would complement and supplement these seed ideas.

We know the power of Christ to regenerate individual lives; now it is possible to witness the power of Christ through biblical reasoning—the principle approach of American Christian education—to renew and govern our curriculum and methods and subsequently develop the self-government necessary to maintain the God-given life, liberty, and property of the American Christian.

## Endnotes

1. Noah Webster, *1828 American Dictionary of the English Language.*
2. Rosalie Slater, *Teaching and Learning America's Christian History* (Foundation for American Christian Education, 1965), 88.
3. *Webster's 1828 Dictionary* definition of the word *seed.*
4. Green pages, Facsimile edition published by the Foundation of American Christian Education, Chesapeake, Virginia.

❋   ❋   ❋

James Rose is a forerunner in the field of American Christian education with over thirty-five years, experience as classroom teacher, headmaster, Bible college professor and chairman of the Department of Education, homeschooling principal, a licensed minister of the gospel, conference speaker, author, compiler, and president of the American Christian History Institute. He conducts rudiments courses, Christian history seminars, and conferences for day school and home-schooled constituents. Presently he is superintendent of the American Christian Academy Extension Campus of Anderson, California, ministering to approximately five hundred home-schooled families and over twelve hundred students in twelve counties of northern California. He is the author of the classical curriculum guide of the principle approach, *A Guide to American Christian Education for the Home and School* (1987).

Rose resides in Millville, California, with his wife, Barbara. They are the parents of four homeschooled children, now ages twenty-one to twenty-seven, and grandparents of four.

# Traditional
# Textbook Method

*There is gold, and a multitude of rubies:*
*but the lips of knowledge are a precious jewel.*

—PROVERBS 20:15

❋   ❋   ❋

*Teaching should be such that what is offered is per-*
*ceived as a valuable gift and not a hard duty.*

—ALBERT EINSTEIN

As parents investigating the methods of education available to homeschool families, many of us wish to find a method that will allow us to throw out what we don't care for from our own educational memories and retain the "good stuff" from the classroom. While we may appreciate the comforting structure found in a textbook or syllabus, do we really want to schedule our family into oblivion, complete with bells that ring every fifty

minutes? Perhaps we want the occasional classroom style inter-
action found in a group of students but not the negative aspects
of having a child stuck with his peers for eight hours a day.
For those who don't know where to start or who want to be
able to take the good from the system, the traditional schoolroom method may be the way to go.

Also referred to as "structured" homeschooling or the
"school-at-home" method, the schoolroom approach is the clos-
est to the standard American schooling system most of us are
familiar with. Gone, however, is the class of thirty or more
students with a harried teacher trying to deal with administra-
tive tasks all day. Instead we find ourselves able to choose from
curriculum providers who offer more or less structure based on
our family's needs. Some "school-at-home" providers offer everything from assessments to tell us what grade level our student
should start with to offering support and encouragement to the
primary teacher in the family. Some provide basic outlines of
lessons to be learned while others require specific time commit-
ments and track completed work in transcripts much as a
traditional private or public school does. Several of the well-
known names in the curriculum catalogs actually offer services
and texts to schools as well as homeschool families, and their
catalogs are full of supplies, from textbooks and science
resources right down to notebooks and pencils! With the traditional schoolroom method, one can literally choose to receive
an entire year's school supplies at the beginning of each school
year. Once the teacher has consulted the goals and resources
for the grade, the child is set on the pathway of learning at
home.

While the traditional method can help an overwhelmed
family find structure and organization, it can also lead to burnout on the part of either the teacher or the students. Having
so many choices is both a joy and a conundrum, as veteran

homeschoolers can attest. As we will hear from Jenefer Igarashi and Dr. Heather Allen of *The Old Schoolhouse Magazine*, there is a wealth of curricula available to families considering the traditional schoolroom approach. Homeschooling mother of five and missionary to Mexico, Jennifer Pepito shares with us the benefits of joining a homeschool co-op for those who wish to bring in the classroom learning environment while still supporting the home education efforts of a family. Should you choose the traditional schoolroom approach, the only thing left to do is decide which curriculum provider best suits your family's needs and educational goals.

# The Traditional
# Schoolroom Approach:
# Bringing the
# Classroom Home

*Jenefer Igarashi and Dr. Heather Allen*

*The traditional schoolroom approach?* Isn't this what homeschoolers have been running from?

Yes, we have been fleeing in huge numbers from modern,
government-funded schoolrooms. However, the schoolrooms
that were set up so many years ago by those first Americans had
noble ideas and God-honoring intentions. David Limbaugh does
a marvelous job at revealing what the traditional schoolroom
was in his book *Persecution* (Regnery). In his book Limbaugh
gives a historical account that most are not aware of. He shared
some of that with *The Old Schoolhouse Magazine* in the Summer
2004 issue: "Ironically, the first common schools in this country
were formed by Christian parents who wanted to make sure
their children learned to read, so that they could read the Bible,
which they believed was essential for salvation."

It reminds me of the Little House on the Prairie books and the school that Laura Ingalls Wilder learned and taught in. What a contrast to our present-day schoolrooms! Today, if one could take away the biased, political-agenda-soaked curriculum; the overwhelmed teachers; age-segregated, overcrowded classrooms; the board who demands that God is checked at the door; the metal detectors, "dumbed-down" lesson plans, and appallingly low academic standards, there would remain a vaguely familiar structure erected by the early Americans with starkly different motives and philosophies, which once served its students well.

When I think of the traditional schoolroom approach, I have grand prospects of recreating, in my own home, what Laura Ingalls Wilder must have been a part of (minus Nellie Olson). Laura Ingalls Wilder not only graduated at age fifteen but also began teaching her own classroom soon after! This maturity and academic standard is what I would like to see with my students. The traditional American schoolroom was a place where God was honored, where high standards were expected, and where the teacher was in control. (Remember *Farmer Boy* where the substitute teacher brought a black whip and lashed the unruly troublemaker right out the door?) The best textbooks available were used, and children of all different ages were taught together.

At this book's inception this poor little section was nearly forgotten. After all, using textbooks and workbooks seems so obvious, yet the sheer immensity of it warrants discussion! The traditional textbook/workbook style is adapted for many reasons. Some of us simply aren't up to the task of sitting down to create volumes of our own homemade curriculum. For others, it is familiar. Textbooks and workbooks are what the general population grew up on. We know what they look like and can use that framework as a model to set up our own homeschool. When used correctly, this method can get the job done successfully!

Many parents, especially those of new homeschool families, find the traditional schoolroom approach one of the easiest methods to implement and use. Had I done a bit more research when I first started homeschooling years ago, it would have been what my family would have used from the beginning. Parents who are fabulously creative or who naturally "think outside the box" are in *heaven* with the limitations shaken away. Not me—be still my pounding heart! When we first began homeschooling, I was overloaded with information. Any homeschooler whom I found I asked, "How do I set this up?" Veteran homeschoolers sang the same glorious praises: "The possibilities are endless, the boundaries are limitless, and the choices of curriculum could fill the deepest sea."

Well, that was my problem! There was just too much to sort through. I was told so many times, "There is no *right* way. You can do whatever works for you!" But my nails were bitten down to jagged little stumps. I didn't know what I was doing; I didn't know what would work for us! I needed a starting point and some guidelines. These are what set programs and set curricula offer. The research has been done; the curriculum has been selected and tested; the guidelines are in place. The recipe has been created and put together. "Just add kid and follow directions." This is the environment my family needed for success; it is why the traditional approach works so well for us.

Many new homeschooling families also appreciate the traditional schoolroom approach because it gives an easy answer to the concerned friends, family, and neighbors who ask, "How do you know what you're doing?" All the footwork has been done, the scope and sequence laid out, and the basic structure of lesson plans set in place. The question, what are they supposed to be learning and when do they need to know it by? is taken care of nicely.

And while we could have cared less about how weird some people thought we were for our educational choices, it would have been reassuring—to the concerned questioners and even to ourselves—to have a set program that had proven success.

However, even with the curriculum chosen, five questions plague many homeschoolers:

- What are the academic standards for my child?
- How do I organize my day?
- What curriculum should I get?
- How do I know if they are succeeding?
- Can I pull this off if I am not disciplined or structured every day?

We are using resources from several different companies (none are paying or have lobbied for this) whom I believe offer highly beneficial programs. We have included "What Worked for Me" stories about how others were able successfully to arrange their homeschool classrooms.

Companies who offer full-grade programs are used in abundance because the major footwork has already been done. When using a planned-out package by a reputable company, beginners feel less shaky about covering all necessary subjects or remaining on track academically with their children's peers.

For the parent who is not starting out with exhilarated confidence, using these programs can bring about great results, personal success, and peace of mind. I sit back with reverent awe of those parents who can charge into their schooling ready to make their own rules and set their own standards. After homeschooling these last years, I can see where I have grown and have become more confident, but I do not believe I could have hung in there without some sort of laid-out structure. Once you learn how to fly, you can spread your wings and test the heights and soar in any direction you want! I've found that as I become more confident, my "home academy" has been molded to our family rather than the other way around. Textbooks and workbooks are also used by those eclectic schoolers who have found "the best of many" different curricula and have put it all together in a way that fits their family's needs. With some of my six children, I mix and match; with the others I use a complete program for all subjects packaged up from one company. I love it!

Before charging right into the personal accounts and reviews of some of the traditional schoolroom programs, let's step back for a moment and see what others have said about some of these programs.

In 2004, *The Old Schoolhouse Magazine (TOS)* conducted a survey of their readers to obtain a snapshot in time, if you will, of their homeschoolers. One of the questions asked focused on the reader's approach to homeschooling and, specifically, what the family's mode of education resembled. Of those responding, 55 percent use an eclectic approach, 21 percent employ a classical approach, 9 percent use traditional methods, and 7 percent use unit studies.

Now, of those 9 percent who use traditional methods, *TOS* wanted to know the specific vendors, or favorite boxed curriculum suppliers, they used. Several of the most frequently mentioned suppliers included A Beka (15 percent), Sonlight (13 percent), Bob Jones University Press (12 percent), Alpha Omega (8 percent), and Saxon (6 percent).

These are interesting statistics, and a starting point, but there is always, like Paul Harvey would say, *the rest of the story.* That is, what makes these statistics interesting and useful to you? We think the answer lies in personal accounts. What better way to gain understanding and a feel for a program than what someone else has to say about it? If you are considering the traditional schoolroom method, relax, read, and see if any of the following strike a chord with you. You might find you are best suited for a traditional schoolroom approach! Remember, there is no right answer, and there is no final answer. Change is allowed.

## Alpha Omega

Christian Program
LIFEPACS: Grades K–12
Horizons: Grades K–6
Switched on Schoolhouse (computer CD programs): Grades 3–12
www.AOP.com

Alpha Omega Publications has made a strong, and well deserved, presence in the homeschool community. Many of us are familiar with their LIFEPACS curriculum; they have been around for twenty-five years!

I first used the LIFEPAC system with one of my six children for the purpose of doing a company curriculum review. The first thought that popped into my head when my LIFEPACS came was *yummy*. Weird? Perhaps, but they reminded me of large boxes of Girl Scout cookies. A distinct advantage to the LIFEPACS program is easy storage. Each subject comes in color-coded boxes and includes an easy-to-handle, spiral bound Teacher's Guide and a series of ten work texts called units. Another noteworthy aspect is the Alpha Omega customer service; I particularly appreciated the online instant messaging help.

The curriculum suited our needs superbly. It was challenging enough and was set up in a way that made it easy to set the year up at a certain pace that worked for us. I liked the versatility of the program. LIFEPACS are a great choice for the student who is self-directed yet works just as well for the one who needs more teacher input as the Teacher Guides include a Curriculum Overview, Management and Structure (directions on how to use the program), Teacher Notes, Alternate Tests with Keys (these are wonderful for practice and reinforcement), Answer Keys, Self Test Keys, and Test Keys. After reviewing the full third grade LIFEPACS program, I chose the Alpha Omega LIFEPACS system for two of my elementary aged children.

## Bob Jones University Press

Christian Programs
Grades K–12
www.bjup.com

Bob Jones University is a tremendous resource for complete curriculum packages. My daughter went through their full ninth-grade program, and we were both pleased with it. The Bob Jones textbooks and teacher's guides do a good job of explaining concepts in the lessons (whether it's math, geography, literature, or physics), and it is easy to set up a day that suits the family's needs. My older children are more self-directed. Because the lessons were explained so well, my daughter rarely ran into snags or had to have me search through the teacher's manuals to clarify the lessons. As a busy mom, I appreciated this. Another thing I appreciate about Bob Jones University Press is that they are so homeschool friendly. Their reps and their company leaders have a true vision for the homeschool community, and they want to be there to serve. As a matter of fact, they were the winners of *The Old Schoolhouse Magazine* 2002 "Friendliest Homeschool Company" award.

## Calvert

Nonsectarian
Grades K–8
www.calvertschool.org

We have been using the Calvert School curriculum for eight years now, covering prekindergarten through sixth grade and currently have three children enrolled. We have also completed many of Calvert's enrichment courses such as King Arthur Through the Ages, Ancient Greece, Spanish I and II, Melody Lane, and Come Read with Me.

The curriculum is comprehensive, interesting, and challenging, and the various grades and enrichment courses are clearly laid out in the catalog. With the Advisory Teaching Service, the program is accredited, and our children have benefited greatly from the feedback they've received from their advisory teachers. Thus far we have been extremely pleased with our experiences with Calvert. When you receive your Calvert curriculum or enrichment course, everything you need is there. Books, paper, pencils, crayons, and rulers: You name it! Especially helpful are the lesson manuals. Every lesson includes an assignment summary, a list of materials, space for notes along the left margin, and step-by-step instructions. This is great if you want to jump right in and get started!

## Christian Light Education

Christian Program
Grades K–12
www.clpcle.com

I was sold on Christian Light Education when we first reviewed copies of their Learning to Read series. I could not wait to see more and contacted Christian Light Education to see what they offer in the way of full-grade programs. I could not have been more impressed. Subjects (and titles) covered in the first-grade program are Bible, language arts, learning to read, reading, mathematics, science, and social studies (optional). Five boxes of flashcards and language arts wall charts were included. Other materials provided were a laminated counting chart and additional practice resource books called *My Counting Book* and *My Calendar Book*.

Each subject came with a Teacher's Guide and a series of Light Unit work texts (similar to Alpha Omega's LIFEPACS) with Self-Checks, Self-Tests, and Unit Test. I found the teacher's manuals to be thorough, easy to understand, and laid out in a simple, clear, step-by-step manner. I did not find myself scratching my head wondering where to find additional materials or having to do any excessive digging to find necessary supplements to complete lessons.

In the lower grade that I examined, CLE seems right on track. There is no push to hurry students along, similarly to the early grade programs from Bob Jones University Press. If you were going from a program such as Alpha Omega's Horizons, or A Beka in the earlier grades, you might consider skipping to the next grade up. My son (whom I consider average or slightly ahead) "grade wise" was in kindergarten when I used the first-grade CLE program, and it was exactly what he needed.

## CLASS

Distance Learning Programs
www.Homeschool.org

Here is another option that appeals to homeschool families. Distance learning programs are essentially private schools. They eliminate the guesswork. The school takes care of the transcripts, records, and report cards; but you, the parent, are in complete control of the school day. Like the other traditional schoolroom companies, distance learning programs send the student curriculum for the school year, but that's just the half of it. Many times (like the CLASS program) your child will take an assessment test, and then the company will choose material to match to the student's level. They are also available for online or phone support. Families who feel like they need a schoolroom structure or perhaps are insecure about the "outside powers that be" find a lot of comfort with programs like these. When my daughter went through a year of the CLASS program, it was nice to respond to those who asked, "So what school do you go to?" that she was enrolled in a private school.

Our year with CLASS was harder academically and a lot more structured than any other program we'd used before. You are expected to keep on track! Students are responsible for getting their work done. Goals and deadlines loom. For our family this was definitely a good thing. My daughter freely admits that while she is an excellent test-taker, she is sorely lacking in discipline, diligence, and self-government when it comes to schoolwork. She jokes that this was the first year she actually completed a textbook, and that's true. I have always had a difficult time in seeing things through, so this was a real lesson in perseverance. Some would argue that setting up a school day in this manner is not really homeschooling; they would argue that the whole essence of homeschooling is that children are learning without pressures from an outside source and not set in a "one size fits all" package. I disagree. We were at home, and she was definitely "schooling," and I really appreciate the skills that were acquired that year. Should she take college courses, she will need many of the habits that she attained while going through this distance learning program.

We encourage families to search out what will work for them and what they are comfortable with. There is a lot of pressure outside, and unfortunately even *inside*, the homeschool community. There are a multitude of homeschooling methods, and people have strong feelings about what is or is not the best. We are a diverse crowd; it's one of the things that make us strong and give us credibility as a group. We're able to think for ourselves and make specific decisions about our children's academics.

A number of companies provide "ready to go" curriculum plans. These reviews offer only an example of what is available! The Internet is a great resource for research, and you can review many curriculum choices in the Product Review pages at *The Old Schoolhouse Magazine* Web site (www.theold school housemagazine.org). When we set upon our homeschool journey, one of the biggest obstacles I faced was self-doubt. I have never met a homeschooler who, right off the bat, had the confidence we assume it must take to be an efficient, capable, and successful teacher. That can be to our benefit. Self-doubt is sometimes the vehicle used to spur on careful research. The more you wonder and learn, the better off you and your student will be. Each family's goals will be different. Our standards will be different. Our styles will be different. But I believe our vision is the same. We are driven by love and by dedication for our children. We want what is best for them and believe that we are capable of knowing what is best for them. Our friends, family, and government may tell us differently. Many would have us believe that public schools or other "professionals" know our children better than we do. My respect to you who have the courage to take on the enormous role of teacher within your family.

Jenefer Igarashi is vice president of operations for *The Old Schoolhouse Magazine* and also writes its quarterly editorial column. Jenefer enjoys being married to her nearly perfect husband, Geoff, and schooling, playing, and laughing with their six kids—that is, when she's not pulling small toys or children out of the toilet, scowling, or bellowing about things being too noisy.

Dr. Heather W. Allen has a Ph.D. in experimental psychology, concentrating on cognition and information processing, human learning and motivation, sensation and perception, and statistics. She also has twenty years' experience as a human factors engineer designing, analyzing, evaluating, and optimizing systems and processes with a focus on the human user.

After serving as an aerospace experimental psychologist in the United States Navy, she worked for Sandia National Laboratories for eleven years in the Statistics and Human Factors Department, the last six of which she held the distinction of Distinguished Member of the Technical Staff. Dr. Allen is respected by her peers as an expert in human factors engineering and has received numerous Awards of Excellence for her work in providing efficient, effective, and practical solutions to her customers.

Heather left the laboratory in 1998 to homeschool her children and to embark on a successful consulting business. Heather has been married to Steve for fifteen years, and for eight years they have homeschooled their four children, Edward, twelve; Joseph, ten; Emily, seven; and Hana, eighteen months. The Allen family resides in Albuquerque, New Mexico.

# Homeschool Co-ops or How Not to Be an Independent Ear

## Jennifer Pepito

OK, you ask, what does my ear have to do with home-schooling? In 1 Corinthians 12, we are given a dynamic picture of how God has granted each of us a special place in his body, which fitted together makes the whole thing work. If you are an ear and you start saying to the nose that you don't need it, you are going to be missing out on some great experiences.

As homeschoolers we are sometimes so fed up with the old way of giving our children to the professionals that we try to become little islands, often missing out on sharing our gifts with others, as well as benefiting from the gifts God has given to the other members of his body.

Now let me give you a picture. Twelve children are sitting around a table in a sunny dining room. They range in age from fifteen all the way down to six. Nearby a few toddlers quietly look at books or simply pull them off shelves, while a mother points out cities on a map of China that the children are working on. Later the children will sit together enjoying yummy broccoli beef and exotic dim sum after listening to each child share a report about that vast country in the east.

One of the mothers has brought a craft for the older children, intricate bamboo strip books, while in a nearby room the small ones are assembling panda bears made of heart-shaped construction paper. This is a history/geography group, and it has greatly enhanced our school in the last few years. The truly wonderful thing about co-ops (or "study groups," as I like to call them) is that there are a million variations to the theme, one for every family.

The first foray we made into the world of co-ops was simply our local support group. They had such things as holiday parties where each parent took on a different aspect of the celebration. Someone did games, there was a story and a craft, and everyone brought some food. My children had the opportunity to join in such memorable childhood favorites as the cakewalk and musical chairs. It also gave them an opportunity to practice good social skills.

The next one, in which our family is continuing, was the science group. Three families get together to do oral reports and science experiments. Each mother takes a turn planning the lesson and hosting. We all agree ahead of time what the main topic of study will be. We are currently studying ponds, and I have been delighted to see my children scoop water out of the creek to try and count critters in their free time. The lesson on life in the pond obviously stuck with them.

The most formal group we have joined has also required the most involvement. For the last few years we have done a living history group; this year our study will focus on non-Western cultures. Four families from our rural area get together in late summer to lay out a year's worth of topics, including designations for who will teach, host, and so on. We have found it works well to rotate the duties every few months to prevent the burnout that might come from having a time-intensive duty such as teaching every week. Because all of us have several other activities we are involved in, we have found it works best to get together once a month. My sister belongs to a similar group that meets every six weeks.

I have found the benefits to our family from these groups to be innumerable. My children have the opportunity to get to know other children of varying ages in a closely supervised setting. One of my daughters thrives on competition; she might have done well in a typical school setting if I had wanted to kill her love of learning and family. I find the groups motivate her to do a better job on reports since they are being presented to a larger audience. Another daughter has some learning differences, so I appreciate her having the opportunity to develop her communication skills in a nonthreatening environment. It has also been helpful to have some ideas of what is normal for her age to see what we are working toward or how far off we are. The groups have also given my preschool children some fun opportunities to do crafts, play games, and listen to stories especially for them. We have all enjoyed getting to spend time with families in our area and hopefully have a small part in "bearing one another's burdens" by being a blessing to one another's children.

The co-ops that I have outlined here only scratch the surface of what is available. Debra Bell, the author of *The Ultimate Guide to Homeschooling* and weekly columnist on The Home School Channel at Crosswalk.com, has a three-part article on her style of co-oping which she calls "Family Schools." As her younger sons entered their teen years, she and a friend brainstormed about how they could meet their children's increasing academic needs. This idea session developed into a family school, which they call CHESS. They meet every Tuesday for five hours, which are divided into one-hour periods. The co-op offers classes for fifth through twelfth graders in literature, composition, and various math and science courses, as well as art, Latin, and Spanish. Most of the teachers are homeschool parents, and they are paid for their services. The family school meets at a church, and each family whose children are involved pays a fee for the classes, around $150 per class. As Debra states in her article, CHESS is in its sixth year and has become the highlight of her homeschool program.

In our local support group some families got together and hired an art teacher for a series of classes. For around five dollars a month, the children received professional art instruction. Another mom I spoke with took her daughter to a Christian Montessori co-op. A few other ladies I know simply swap their kids for a refreshing, kid-free day to plan and do necessary errands. The possibilities are endless.

So how do you go about starting a co-op? Well, the first question to ask is, "What do I feel is lacking in my routine?" For me it was the hands-on projects; for a parent with older children, it may be higher-level math or science. Would you like your kids to be in an art history class? Ask around. Chances are there is someone feeling the same way and someone who could teach it. If you are not a part of a local support group, join one now! Homeschool support groups are a great place to network.

Once you find others who share your interest, get together at someone's house for tea and planning, preferably in the evening while the kids are at home with hubby or a grandparent. We have always been blessed with easy and straightforward meetings. The ladies usually come with some particular thing they enjoy doing or want to accomplish, and we brainstorm about how to achieve it. After the initial meeting the mom in charge of the schedule types it up and mails it to everyone. During the year we have occasionally had to tweak a schedule, but it is helpful to know your responsibilities ahead of time. We have never charged for our group. Since we rotate responsibilities, the costs seem to spread out evenly, and we prefer to keep things simple. It's all about what works for the families in your homeschool community.

I am so thankful that God has led us into this phenomenal way of homeschooling. We still make it our ambition to be home, leading a quiet life, but the benefits to my children and myself have been endless. Across the country people are getting excited about a method that doesn't supersede their core principles or style. You can still be a classical educator, do unit studies, or use the traditional textbook approach. What co-oping does is help us to be accountable to one another and give our children the opportunity to build relationships and skills with their extended family, God's family, while continuing to protect and encourage the immediate family God has placed us in.

☀   ☀   ☀

Jennifer Pepito is the homeschooling mother of five children. She enjoys writing, reading good books, and encouraging women to love their husbands and their children. She and her husband Scott are currently in the process of moving to Mexico to do full-time mission work. After four idyllic years in the Sierra Nevada foothills, they feel the hand of God leading them to Baja to work with the many Mexican Indians toiling in the farms there. While in the U.S., Jennifer has enjoyed many wonderful experiences learning with other homeschool families, and she looks forward to the new experiences her family will have co-oping with the Holy Spirit, other missionaries, and native Mexicans to share the love of Christ.

# Charlotte Mason
# Method

* * * * * * * * * * * * * * * * * * * * * * * *

*And that ye study to be quiet, and to do your
own business, and to work with your own hands,
as we commanded you.*

—1 THESSALONIANS 4:11

※　※　※

*Children need opportunities for unstructured play—
swinging on the swings and throwing rocks and
playing with basketballs. . . . Education is a vitally
important part of our children's lives, but it is only
one part. Balance between these competing objectives
is the key word.*

—JAMES DOBSON

Families searching for the middle ground between a child-centered teaching method and a solid educational track often turn to the writings of nineteenth-century educator Charlotte Mason. This approach, also known as the "living books" method, incorporates "whole" books and literature rather than dry textbooks. It offers a firm foundation in core academic subjects (reading, writing, and math) while also exploring the arts and nature in depth. Narration makes use of the child's natural urge to share what they've learned to help reinforce their knowledge of various subjects. This process allows for a dialogue between the student and teacher wherein questions about materials and further teaching about a family's beliefs can be shared.

Known for short lessons and a focus on establishing good habits, this method encourages structured families to remain organized while still allowing for variance based on children's ages and maturity levels. The length of time dedicated to studies expands as the child grows but still allows for free time for personal pursuits. Even high school-aged students will be done with their lessons early enough in the day to be involved with other activities such as church and community service, pursuit of hobbies and other activities. Throughout the entire education process students are exposed to reinforcement of good habits such as attentiveness, imagining, and better memory.

Nature walks are another prominent feature in the Charlotte Mason approach. The creation of nature notebooks after such forays allows children not only to experience God's world firsthand but also to save and revisit their experiences through the use of drawings, poetry, and identification of flora and fauna encountered. Frequent nature walks allow the entire family to see the cycles of the seasons and changes in their environment due to human activity. Even homeschoolers located in urban areas can participate in this process as they become more observant of their natural surroundings and how plants and animals adapt and thrive in such locations. Such activities also provide a method of showing how various academic subjects are so often interrelated. As students observe nature and participate in outdoor activities, they can cover science, language arts, artistic efforts, and the obvious physical education involved in walks or hikes.

Homeschoolers using the Charlotte Mason method are often exuberant about their "teacher" and her approach. After hearing from renowned author and speaker Catherine Levison, you may well feel like you've found the method for your family.

# The Charlotte Mason Method

## Catherine Levison

There are literally millions of homeschoolers, and sometimes it seems like there are millions of choices to be made, especially when first introduced to all of the alternatives available. I remember the strain and the unexpected negative emotions I encountered when first homeschooling. Everybody had an idea or something to sell, and I contemplated every single one of them. Finally, I had to choose and actually begin the home education process. I kept one goal foremost in my mind during those early months, but it soon lost its meaning for me. I knew I needed a far more meaningful goal.

Burnout hit me hard, and it hit me early. I was already calling private schools and investigating bus routes after one year of homeschooling. To tell you the truth, I went all the way to having my children enrolled after meeting with the potential teachers who would be assuming the responsibility of educating my children. While waiting for September to come along, I learned something important about making decisions: sometimes by making the wrong choice and not being able to live with the consequences, you are then able to see the correct course to take. My peace of mind was restored when I canceled the enrollment and turned my attention back to homeschool. However, I knew that the original materials and the method I had chosen had to be replaced by something I could actually enjoy using.

Charlotte Mason's name was far more obscure back in those days, but I was able to visit a small school that used her techniques solely. I went to their open houses and parents meetings, read their planning strategies, and generally picked the brains of the small faculty. Soon I was reading Charlotte Mason's six-volume educational set. I liked what I read there, but time was of the essence. Many have found, as I did, that the six volumes she wrote were largely philosophical, but one individual who was connected to the CM school helped tremendously with this problem. She frequently flew across the country in a continuous effort to photocopy decades of the *Charlotte Mason* magazine from the Library of Congress. This monthly periodical contained the practical, hands-on data necessary to use the CM method. With this kind of reading material, I was able to start a Charlotte Mason-based education at home.

As skeptical and untrained as I was in the method, I decided simply to try one technique at a time. I continued to use the textbook-style method while I experimented. I worked up to a half-and-half style of homeschooling, but it was the Charlotte Mason stuff that worked. I was pleasantly surprised as the children enjoyed each and every new thing we did. I was also pleasantly surprised when the drudgery, the burnout, and the shear dread went away. Enjoying yourself isn't the only goal though; a thorough education is also important, so I watched that carefully too. At the end of this mixture year, I held an all Charlotte Mason summer school session at home. As a family, we had a blast; and the academics, the retention, and the lasting knowledge were there for us too. In fact we learned far more that summer than we had using a more traditional textbook method.

Amid all of the new techniques, some of which I'll be detailing for you shortly, I had developed a whole new goal for my homeschool. While Charlotte Mason wrote about many things, caught on to her emphasis of the children having a love for learning. When I made this my priority, I found that everything changed. It's important to have goals that hold meaning for you, and this particular one has meant a lot to me. Everything I do, buy, and use is evaluated based on whether it develops a love for learning or kills the love for learning. My materials, books, games, and approaches had to contain an anti-boredom feature. Thanks to Mason, I was selecting challenging, interesting items to use and subjects to cover. She taught homeschooling parents and classroom teachers never to underestimate the intelligence of the child and purposefully to choose topics and books that might stretch them beyond what would normally be expected.

Burned-out parents surrounded me everywhere I went. Their hearts were in homeschooling, and they loved their children endlessly, but they appeared unhappy and uninspired. Many times the tissue box was passed around at a local support group meeting I attended, and while I too shared some of the frustration they felt so intensely, I was different in my overall demeanor. I must have stood out as the well-adjusted one, and eventually the leader asked me to take an entire meeting to share my secrets—my "Charlotte Mason" thing. That night led to constant invitations to talk at support group meetings and to lead one of my own groups. I saw that the effects of the Charlotte Mason methods were beneficial to parents around me, and their enthusiasm was contagious. Oddly enough this was happening all over the country; many speakers, authors, and homeschool groups were bringing the Charlotte Mason method into the top ten in terms of popularity.

Why did it catch on as it did? I think seeing is believing, and parents everywhere were putting the CM concepts into action. Some practice a CM-only style while many others combine it with other methods. Personally, I've always advocated any combination of styles that work for you in your own home. I used a textbook/CM combo for a while, so I know that works. I've recommended people go ahead and combine it with the unit study approach, the unschooling (or relaxed) style, or even a classical education. I really do believe any amount of Charlotte Mason a family wants to use will work.

My work in the homeschooling arena has always involved telling people exactly how to use the Charlotte Mason method and make it as practical as I possibly could. Assuming you're busy and would like to spend more time doing the method than researching it, I wrote books that get parents right into it.

I'd like to share as much as I can with you in this book—things you can try at home and see how they work with your children. Starting with narration, you'll find it's one of many techniques that can be used in lots of situations no matter what style of homeschooling you ultimately choose.

Narration is a simple matter of repeating what you know. The act of repeating is powerful in its own right; it helps to assimilate the newly acquired information while activating the brain's memory. Plus, the parent can detect instantly whether the child heard the information—a big bonus with giving directions or chore lists to kids. For example, next time you want a child to clean the basement, sweep the stairs, and feed the dog, ask him to tell you what you just said. That'll end the old "I didn't hear you, Mom."

For educational purposes the applications are endless. One common use of narration is to read a short section of any type of written material. This can be done aloud to a group of children or completed individually through silent reading. Afterward, the child verbally narrates what he just read. In a group choose one volunteer and have only that one child narrate. All you have to do is listen and look interested, knowing all the while that different minds will have different reactions. Practice makes perfect, and this being a normal brain function, it does come easily to most people.

We usually start this practice at the age of six, but you can allow younger children to join in as well. Written narrations begin at the age of ten. The same format can be used—a short reading followed by a written rendition of what they just learned. You can also use the dictation method, meaning the child speaks and you write. This is especially effective using a computer where they can watch their words appear on the monitor. Something important is learned through this since writing is similar to speaking, and this will take a lot of the fear out of the writing process as the child matures.

Time frames are unimportant with narration. You can spend days, weeks, or months on any topic and then ask the child to tell (or write) everything he or she now knows about the subject. Charlotte Mason schools asked for narrations daily and at the end of each trimester required the child to assimilate data from the previous several weeks.

Subject matter can be varied. Practice narration after written material, documentaries, field trips, and math lessons. It can completely take the place of testing and in the long run is a far more positive experience. Winston Churchill once said of testing, "I should have liked to be asked to say what I knew. They always tried to ask what I did not know. When I would have willingly displayed my knowledge, they sought to expose my ignorance."

Listening is a valuable skill to have in relationships and employment. It's also a kind, polite skill to be able to use. Narration will help your children become both skilled listeners and the type of persons whose reading comprehension is far above normal. Written narrations are excellent practice for the essay, something still required at the college level, plus the children will expand their rhetoric skills, a great asset to adult life.

Art appreciation is another simple matter in the Charlotte Mason method. To try it yourself, get a piece of art from a calendar, large coffee-table book, or whatever you can find. Have the children look at the art quietly for a few minutes, remove the art from their sight, and have them describe the picture to you verbally. Every child gets a turn with this, starting with the youngest child. I was so awestruck the first time I tried this that I thought I'd need to be revived from a faint! It worked from the start, and we loved it. My kids were able to describe the art as accurately as if they were looking at it. In fact, if you have a less-abled child, allow him or her to look at it while describing it, then he or she can participate as well as the other children.

We collected inexpensive prints everywhere we went to enlarge our collection, and we borrowed art books from the library. We approached the artist's work in a random fashion whereas the CM schools were more systematic. They choose an artist and view (study) only their work once a week for six weeks before moving on to another artist. It is recommended that as the children age they write down their descriptions and file them in a notebook. Some even keep a photocopy of the art adjacent to the description. Another thing older children do with this idea is to create their own sketch of the art after the short observation time. Again, the art is out of sight during this time.

Nature sketching was another big hit at our house, and it opened a whole new world for me. First, I hadn't been going outside enough—a habit I then developed thanks to Charlotte Mason's strong convictions in this area. By providing each child and myself with a sketchbook and heading out the door, we improved our observation skills 200 percent. Go to a park, arboretum, or your own yard and sketch the objects you find. If the weather is bad, bring home some samples and throw them on a table for sketching indoors later. The sketched specimens can be labeled in English and/or Latin, dated or noted by the locale in which they were found. Poems or scientific data can augment the books too. Some people record science experiments in their books as well as the time of day the sun is setting. Because they are also called *nature diaries* or *nature journals*, they can be used daily or weekly. We always had a lot of fun taking the journals on vacation because we'd usually be somewhere completely different from our climate, and that would mean we could journal new leaves, birds, and insects. My children became so observant that one time I showed them a picture in a science book and without warning had them sketch what they had seen. The results were unbelievable, and I think it was due to the nature sketching and the art study. Observant children are great.

Short lessons provide the time necessary to do some of these things I've described. Charlotte Mason believed in an invigorating, quick-paced morning full of varied topics. Using small increments of time, a schedule is followed attempting to use opposites. Passive practice lessons that take little thought because the concepts are already understood are interspersed with new concept teachings that require deep thinking. Fun and enjoyable activities that take more movement are followed by quieter lessons such as reading.

Keeping the brain active and engaged is the main goal; also children perform best when they know exactly what is asked of them and how long they have to complete the task. Literally, short lessons are fifteen to twenty minutes for the elementary years and thirty to forty-five minutes for junior and senior high students. It's a structured morning, making for a structured week of school where everything gets covered: time for algebra, grammar, foreign language, art study, nature walks, spelling—all of it has a set time allotted. The child goes from math to poetry, from spelling to art, and they are actually refreshed during the process.

This type of scheduling is not too labor intensive for the parent as you need to create only one and follow it as long as you choose. We actually use a timer during short lessons, and the kids like to try to beat the timer to the end of their math or whatever subject they're working. It's like a game show to them.

If you find this concept to be the opposite of relaxed homeschooling, you're half right. But consider this, all afternoon, all evening, and all weekend are free for both the kids and yourself. The short lessons typically end around lunch, and then everybody can follow his or her own interests and hobbies at any chosen pace. Mom is guilt free because she's had a thorough homeschool day. She knows she covered important topics like science, phonics, and grammar; and now she can enjoy herself the rest of the day. Children get to be children, which was important to Charlotte Mason due to the brevity of childhood, but they've covered more than the basic elements of a standard education. Even subjects they hate have to be studied, and knowing that math is a set time each day and won't be back until tomorrow is reassuring to the child. I find a structured morning followed by an unstructured afternoon to be the best compromise between unschooling (or relaxed, interest led) and a rigorous "school at home" format.

Self-education is another attribute of the CM method. Short lessons help teach children many things about life including the fact that *only they can learn* the material. Mom can't jump into the little body and make it think, as much as she'd like to be able to do that for them. Schedules and timers create enough structure that as the children age they can then settle themselves down and concentrate adequately enough to comprehend what they're covering. Truthfully, the timer and schedule will become unnecessary over time because self-education starts to take over, and habits begin to form.

Habit, you'll find, is another crucial Charlotte Mason teaching. She noted, as did the early Greeks, that we are creatures of habit. She used many examples when writing about habits, but I like to use driving to illustrate the point. Have you ever driven your car to the store so deep in thought that you kind of woke up and found yourself there? How did you do that? Do you realize you had at least two pedals, two mirrors, many windows and massive amounts of hand-to-eye coordination going simultaneously? Not to mention the navigation process—not only did you find your destination, but you also didn't collide with anything on the way. We are habitual. We eat, bathe, shop, think, and even talk out of habit. Knowing and applying this to homeschool works well.

Just as the Greeks did, Charlotte said to target one bad habit at a time and replace it with a new habit. The new habit ordinarily takes six weeks to cement, and then it's just that—a habit. Choose another, allow another six weeks, and soon enough you'll have children who get out of bed and make the bed immediately, without a conflict; children who clear their messes from the kitchen table; children who sit down ready for school; or children who have actually broken the habit of giving you a hard time each morning. Sound miraculous? It's not. It's a simple recognition of human nature, and we are using it to our advantage. Charlotte Mason wrote a lot about this because it does work and it is powerful. I doubted the extreme to which she took this teaching for years, but time and time again I saw in my own behavior that there is a lot of truth to the entire concept. Try it for yourself, and if it doesn't work, then don't use it. The same thing goes for short lessons themselves. For years I've said to parents, "Try it; if it does not work for you, go back to the long lessons or whatever method did work in your home."

Books and literature cannot be avoided when giving a brief Charlotte Mason synopsis. Other literary-based homeschool methods are available, but none of them inspired me as much to locate and use the best books ever written. Book selection is one of many critical aspects to this method, as it should be in any homeschool approach or philosophy. For every well-written work on dolphins or President Lincoln, there are probably hundreds of badly written books on the same topic. Charlotte Mason thought that the books themselves had to be interesting and that gifted writers who cared about their topic were more likely to put their whole heart into their projects. Books were scarce in her day, and to have a book-filled life and education were of the utmost importance. Reading Shakespeare, Aristotle, Goethe, Plutarch, Thomas Carlyle, Robert Louis Stevenson, and Charles Dickens are routine in the Charlotte Mason home-schools. Raising the bar and helping to create well-read children is fun and rewarding.

As with much of the CM ideals and practices, I found my own knowledge growing with each new introduction to a fabulous author, whether it was a piece of fiction or nonfiction. This in itself is such a relief and serves as an anti-burnout factor—learning along with your children new things that you never covered in school. Incidentally, this is why a Charlotte Mason parent spends so much time reading aloud to her children—we want to present adult-level reading material at a young age. Reading the classics is enjoyable for the parent due to the quality of the sentence structure and the stories that have withstood the test of time. Children are exposed to imagination-capturing books with high vocabulary that will expand their minds, increase their reading ability, and inspire them to become better writers. Good literary taste is a highly desirable trait in a person; and once achieved, it will be similar to preferring fine French pastries over stale convenience store doughnuts. You and your family will probably find yourselves unable to return to the dumbed-down, poorly written books that are so plentiful in today's market.

Another huge aspect of the CM method is the use of the humanities and the liberal arts. If well-educated children are your goal, you will want to think in terms of broad, generous, or—in other words—liberal. Using short lessons will enable you to study composers, artists, poets, and their work. Geography, geology, history, and all of the mathematics are also included in a generous, liberal education. Any and all of the sciences are included, as are physical exercise, foreign language (up to four or five at a time if you want to be just like Charlotte Mason), and a massive concentration on history. The key concept here is to broadly educate a young person and then allow him or her to pursue a specialty in the field of their choice. Here we have yet another reason this method advanced in popularity among homeschoolers.

To be realistic, homeschooling involves covering a lot of mundane subjects such as teaching kids how to read, multiply, the capitol cities—all things you already know. This is why home-schooling can be tedious work at times. However, if learning French for the first time yourself while teaching it to your children can raise your interest level, then you have a lasting motivation. For me there was the entire history of the world that I had no knowledge of. In my day social studies had replaced history. Consequently, every single thing we covered as a family was new to me. Since I was ignorant and untaught in so many areas, I had no problem choosing a topic and going after it like there was no tomorrow. Once we got into European history, we spent at least four years covering it. When we turned our attention to our own country, we found that our more complete background in European history made us appreciate U.S. history in a whole new way.

In closing, you will, if you haven't already, hear some of the key Charlotte Mason slogans being used, as they have become famous. They are actually mottoes she chose to influence the children and the teachers in her schools. For the parents and teachers she chose, "Education is an atmosphere, a discipline, a life," and for the children she chose, "I am, I can, I ought, I will." These you find on her gravestone, along with "For the Children's Sake." Someone thought these sayings were important enough that they should permanently mark her grave. An acquaintance and great admirer of hers wrote this of her: "When she talked with you, she brought out the best that was in you, something that you did not know was there. She caught you up to her level, and for the time you stayed there; and you never quite fell back again."

I personally never quite fell back again. Her ideas, thoughts, and techniques changed how I educated my children and myself. I'll never be the same, and I am grateful. As I once wrote before, when I feel like giving up, I am motivated by these words of Charlotte Mason: "What the spring is to the year, school days are to our life . . . because that which we get in our youth we keep through our lives."

❄   ❄   ❄

Catherine Levison, mother of five, began homeschooling in the late eighties. Concerned about the quality of education, she selected the Charlotte Mason method. Her family flourished due to creative and effective techniques combining the humanities with consistent attention to academics.

Catherine decided to help others learn how to home educate happily. Her goal has been to give practical advice while encouraging parents to think for themselves and develop a style that personally suit them.

Catherine currently resides in Seattle, Washington. Catherine's book titles include *A Charlotte Mason Education: A Home Schooling How-to Manual* and *More Charlotte Mason Education: A Home Schooling How-to Manual.* Her latest book is *A Literary Education: An Annotated Book List.*

# Unit Study
# Method

* * * * * * * * * * * * * * * * * * * *

*Shew me thy ways, O LORD; teach me thy paths.*
*Lead me in thy truth, and teach me.*

—PSALM 25:4–5

✳ ✳ ✳

*I cannot comprehend the neglect of a family library in*
*such days as these.*

—JANE AUSTEN

Homeschool parents who are looking for a way to integrate lessons for students of varying ages and abilities often turn to unit studies for answers. The unit study approach allows a family to be structured or flexible in their method of teaching while still covering the bases on academic subjects. Using a single theme for planning activities and lessons offers the teacher and students the opportunity to use their various interests and passions to discover, learn, and retain the subject matter.

Because units of study can be chosen based on the overall interest of the family (or child), or to reach goals for study based on grade levels, the themes can vary widely from family to family. While one homeschool family will focus on an interest in frogs to create learning opportunities suddenly for a student about all things amphibian, another may choose to select themes for the school year in advance, with special consideration to holidays and future travel plans. Some families allow older students to create their own units of study, allowing them to focus on hobbies, interests, or academic requirements for future educational efforts such as college admissions. Larger families may also pair older children with younger counterparts to allow for the passing on of wisdom from the older to the younger and the opportunity to serve and learn parenting and teaching skills for the older student.

Even with the amount of variety from family to family and from one theme to the next, unit studies as a whole normally incorporate a few key concepts. Rather than breaking down the theme into small chunks of isolated information or subjects, the unit study method allows learners to see the connectedness of subjects through the overall theme. The ability to focus on topics of interest to the student(s) or teacher creates a more impassioned learning process; in return the students are more likely to retain the information for future recollection. While some parents choose to purchase prewritten units, others use the unit study method as a way of stretching their budget. Using the local library for reading material, theme-related field trips on free "educator days" and borrowing resources from other families with a shared passion can help stretch a homeschool parent's dollar much further. Lastly, for families with children at various age, grade, or cognitive levels, the unit study method allows for accommodation and adjustment of the curriculum resources to each child's ability level.

Whether you are seeking to create your own unit studies for an entire school year, wish to supplement a standard curriculum with a summer learning option, or are trying to figure out the way to choose an effective unit study package for your family, our next quests offer many answers. We'll now learn from Jessica Hulcy of KONOS and Jennifer Steward of Steward Ship. Each of these experts offer ways to use the unit study method effectively in the homeschool.

# Unit Studies

## Jessica Hulcy

When I was a young girl, my father took our family on monthlong vacations across the United States. Since we traveled with four hundred *National Geographic* magazines in the backseat of our station wagon, these trips were more than vacations; these trips were both fun and educational.

Somehow, on these treks across America, my father showed me the connectedness of all the subjects in the world. Monticello wasn't just about the man Thomas Jefferson. Monticello embodied architecture in the buildings, botany in the gardens, history in Jefferson's political achievements, and a worldview of how men should be treated in the written words of the Declaration of Independence.

I wanted to impart this same connectedness of the world to my children when I began homeschooling, so I chose unit studies as the connector of subjects. Under unit themes, subjects fit together, giving them meaning. If "trust" is the theme, our focus is on sheep trusting their shepherd for their every need. Children memorize Psalm 23 (Bible); examine similes, metaphors, and analogies in Psalm 23 (English); study the habits

and traits of sheep (science); research the actual responsibilities
and duties of a shepherd (history); read the Newberry Award
winner . . . *And Now Miguel,* which is the story of a shepherd
boy's life (literature); card, spin, and weave sheep's wool (art);
and lastly, write a paper entitled "From Sheep to Shawl" (writing). Units connect a multitude of topics through a theme.

The unit study method of home education has fringe benefits that go beyond teaching the "connectedness" of things.
My children retain information and facts because factual data
hangs together in nice tidy packages. But the greatest bonus
from doing units is the sense of learning, reading, and doing
together as a family. There is a sense of family connectedness
in addition to the factual connectedness.

Academics are important, but relationships are even more
important. Units help build those treasured relationships between
family members that last a lifetime. This is what my father gave
me, and this is what I now give my children.

## What Are Unit Studies All About?

F. Scott Fitzgerald once said, "The test of first-rate intelligence is the ability to hold two opposing ideas in the brain at
the same time and still retain the ability to function."
Homeschooling moms not only qualify for "first-rate intelligence," but they could probably run IBM on the backstroke.
In the morning moms juggle a myriad of subjects and age
levels as math, reading, and language arts are taught. However,
in the afternoon, unit studies allow moms to stop juggling as
the entire family gets together on the same page, on the same
topic.

## Units Integrate Subjects for Retention and Understanding

My mouth begins to salivate at the smell of chocolate, the sight of gorgeous wallpaper, and the thought of a tightly woven unit. Studying a unit on attentiveness means studying a people whose lives depended on being attentive: American Indians. Using a United States map, children draw in the varying regions where the differing groups of Indians lived. This forces the children to actually practice the main topic of the unit, attentiveness, and they are attentive to the distinctives of the different Indian groups. Children build a fire without matches, cook and eat pemmican balls, read "Hiawatha" by Henry Wadsworth Longfellow and *The Trail of Tears* by John Ross, construct a travois for their dog to pull, learn sign language, dance Indian dances, sandpaint, throw a clay pot, carve a totem pole, research Geronimo and Chief Joseph, and finally, write a paper comparing how the Plains Indians depended entirely on the buffalo while the Northwest Indians depended entirely on the cedar tree for their existence. Geography, poetry, literature, art, dance, cooking, construction, research, and writing are all used to study one topic.

By using all subjects to point back to a topic, the topic is reinforced over and over. By using all senses to experience a topic, the topic is reinforced again and again. Repetition builds retention. It also creates the big picture memory file for topics, thus giving students fuller understanding of the topic they studied.

## Units Challenge Students at Their Own Level

A great Bible teacher, Henrietta Mears, once said, "God put the wiggle in children. Don't you dare try to take it out." As mother of four boys, that statement was a great relief to me.

I could use the wiggle for my boys to learn instead of tying them to the chair. We could all sit round the kitchen table and talk about the seasons while we are studying a unit on orderliness.

However, talk is cheap. Much more memorable is to ask one child to dress for winter, another to dress for summer, and others to dress for fall and spring. The winter dresser wears snowsuit, muffler, cap and mittens, ice skates, and holds a cup of hot chocolate, while the summer dresser dons bathing suit, flip-flops, sunglasses, carries a beach towel and ball, and holds a glass of iced lemonade. Getting children up and out of their chairs capitalizes on rather than fights against the springs in young children's bottoms.

Most parents see the clear benefits of doing activities. They realize no one learns computer skills without the computer. However, parents are concerned that each child be challenged to his level. A single activity serves as the starting point, the vehicle for challenging each child to his personal level. The activity is like a bus ride, with each child getting off at a different stop.

In an attentiveness unit, ears and eyes, Helen Keller and Louis Braille, sound and music, and many more subjects are studied. A great activity is to dissect a cow's eyeball. The younger child simply dissects the eyeball and names the parts. The middle child dissects, names the parts, draws the parts, and takes apart a discarded camera with older brother. The oldest does everything the younger children did but goes one step further by writing a paper comparing how the eye and the camera work. The starting point for each child is a single activity, yet each child is challenged to his own level, getting off the bus at his own stop.

## Discovery Learning Creates Thinkers

Discovery learning is more than activities. It is activities plus kids thinking and kids testing what they think.

When classifying rocks in the orderliness unit, traditional teachers hold up a piece of feldspar and ask the child to repeat the name and then test to see if the child remembered. Much better is to give the child a canvas bag, hammer, chisel, and goggles, and then turn him loose to collect, test, and identify his own rocks.

Discovery allows children to figure things out for themselves, practicing the process of thinking. Teaching children the way God designed them, full of motion, while urging them to think and test what they think yields wiggly thinkers.

## Units Build Relationships and Families

Having birthed four wiggly thinkers, I teach units in self-defense. It is necessary for me to teach all that I can to as many as I can at the same time to keep from being institutionalized.

Besides preserving my sanity, units allow our whole family to learn together. Textbook-based education separates us, even when more innovative resources such as videos and computer software are used. Picture three children using traditional curricula. While one child is watching a biology video in the living room, another is in the kitchen writing a paper on weather, and still another is reading about rocks in his room. Talk about a fragmented family—different rooms and different subjects!

Bible, science, history, literature, art, and music can be rolled together in multilevel units allowing families actually to come back to the same room and study the same topic. Units allow older children to read to younger children, to set up activities for younger children, and to teach younger children. This is great parental training for the older child and builds togetherness in the family.

There is a real temptation in the homeschooling movement to adopt classroom-teaching methods using only workbook and textbook, tell-and-regurgitate teaching methods. Certainly parents can point to stacks of filled-in workbook pages, but the real questions are: Did the child understand what he wrote? Does he know in his mind what he studied? And can he apply it to real life?

Units offer retention of material covered, challenge to individual potential, and room to think for oneself. Not only can a mother stay sane, but she can also enjoy her afternoons with her family all on the same subject, all in the same room.

## How to Avoid Mindless Unit Studies

I am often asked, "How do you think up such creative units?" I must admit, units, though not exactly genetic to me, were bred into my very fabric by my theme-oriented mother. I grew up in a home where everything matched. If we had crepes for dinner, we dined to "The Last Time I Saw Paris." A bowl of chili was eaten to the strains of "The Yellow Rose of Texas" with bandanna napkins and a centerpiece complete with miniature Texas flags and cacti. Matching was not limited to the culinary realm. It extended to color-coordinated Christmas decorations, theme birthday parties, and even matching sister dresses for special occasions for my sisters and me.

As I absorbed the "make-it-match mentality" in my own home, I often became frustrated with my theme if it did not work out to the ninth degree. There was the fireman birthday party complete with fire truck cake, fireman party hats, and a ride on a fire truck, yet I could not find cheap fire trucks for favors. I could not be satisfied with just *any* toy car. After all, four-year-olds would notice, wouldn't they? Or the Winnie the Pooh party where "pin the tail on Eeyore the donkey" fit nicely, but woe be to my poor husband who suggested the game of dropping clothespins in a milk bottle. "Where in any of the Pooh stories was there ever a mention of milk bottles or clothespins?" I retorted.

Small wonder when I began teaching, my mind thought in units. But just as having a panic attack over fire truck favors edged on the ridiculous, so some units can verge on the ridiculous. Some units seem to be contrived instead of flowing together naturally. Here are three red flags to beware of in units.

## Beware of Units That Miss the Big Picture

If a unit revolves around American history, *The Witch of Blackbird Pond* is a natural book to read. If the unit launches off into pond life, for the sake of adding science to the unit, then the entire point of the book has been lost as well as the point of the unit. *The Witch of Blackbird Pond* is about Puritan history, tolerance and intolerance, obedience and disobedience, love and hate, not about pond life. For a unit to be well constructed, each activity should contribute to the big picture rather than strain at minutia or incidentals. All activities should build on the same general theme, rounding out the unit. Units should be as carefully woven as fabric is woven. It makes no sense to be weaving with yarn and then to insert a piece of barbed wire.

## Beware of Units That Integrate Every Subject in Every Unit

Sometimes integrating every subject in every unit simply does not work. A unit on air pressure should not force art into the unit just to check art off the list of subjects covered. While an art activity such as "paint or draw air" is a definite waste of time, another art activity to paint with a straw is not a waste of time. As the child sucks paint into the straw, places his finger over the end of the straw, and then releases his finger and slings paint on the paper, he is using the principle of air pressure he has just learned. This art activity reinforces the main theme of the unit. Let's face it. Some units are heavy on science or history while other units are heavy on art or music. Many moms are frustrated when they cannot have thirty minutes of each subject balanced perfectly in each unit. This attitude causes the natural flow of a unit to be lost.

## Beware of Units That Have No Higher Purpose

Christians should teach children not only units of *what* but also units of *why*. All knowledge should further our understanding of God as well as equip us to operate in the world. Units on simple machines, inventions, and the Industrial Revolution should emphasize the common character traits of the inventors such as resourcefulness and persistence. Children should focus on the character traits of those they study. While studying grains and bread, parents should point children to "the Bread of life," which is in the Word of God, and to the bread of Communion to crack open a door of wonderment revealing an incredible God of orderliness, creativity, and design.

Pointing to a higher purpose need not be contrived. Beyond all facts, figures, and activities is the Creator of the universe whom we want our children to know personally. The more Christian parents study his Word, the more we will see it evidenced in everything from gardening to Beethoven, and the more we will pass this wonder on to our children.

At KONOS we have a saying: *The whole library is our textbook, and the whole world is our curriculum.*

This is the curriculum God lays before us. It is his curriculum that provides one giant unit study perfectly connected and woven together for us to enjoy.

❋   ❋   ❋

Jessica Hulcy, coauthor of KONOS curriculum, is an educator, an author, a popular national homeschool speaker, and a homeschooling mom of four sons. A graduate of the University of Texas at Austin in English/biology with postgraduate work in zoology/education at East Texas State University, Jessica taught five years in underprivileged areas in Dallas public schools. It was there she learned the value of the hands-on, discovery learning method of teaching.

Jessica and husband Wade live in Anna, Texas, on seventy-five acres where Jessica continues homeschooling their youngest son, writing curriculum, and leading yearly KONOS tours to Europe.

# Unit Study Method

*Jennifer Steward*

L et's talk about homeschooling. OK, so you're thinking, *I thought we were going to talk about unit studies.* Well, we are, but hold on for just a moment while we look at the Big Picture of *why* we educate our children at home. If home education is important to us, we need to find the best method for our family and one that we can use successfully. Home-schooling offers many benefits and opportunities, and one obvious benefit is academic advancement. However, probably the largest benefit would be that of training our children in godliness and building godly character into them. Though we feel the unit study method is a desirable approach, our real goal in using unit studies ourselves, and also teaching others about this method, is twofold. First, we believe the method enables students to develop a true love for learning and gain a real education full of delight and interest instead of merely going through the motions and jumping through required academic hoops. Second, we feel that learning how to use this method will enable parents to meet with success in their homeschooling. In other words, you will be able to accomplish teaching your children in such a way that they not only learn better and retain more but also actually love it.

If you are able to continue and not get discouraged and don't have to put up with grumbling students, you will find yourself working with a method that you can carry out without an extreme amount of effort or work. You will enjoy teaching and learning yourself, and then you will not give up. The Bible says, "Let us not become weary in doing good, for at the proper time we will reap a harvest if we do not give up" (Gal. 6:9 NIV). We believe children will be more likely to stay close to the faith, growing to maturity and fulfilling God's purpose in their lives, if we do not give up! We want to help give you the tools not only to give your children the best you can give them but also to ensure that you do not give up!

Let's take a look at two friends. Renee and Marie each homeschool their children. After several frustrating years of homeschooling, Renee and her family have finally discovered the joy of learning through unit studies! Renee notices her friend struggling and tries to encourage Marie by saying, "Why don't you try doing a unit study? Unit studies have made a huge difference in our schooling!"

Marie's response is typical. "Ahhh! Me? I don't have the energy, creativity, or the time to plan a unit study! And besides, I don't know how to sew costumes!" Somewhere along the line, Marie has heard that the unit study method is work intensive for mom. Unit studies have a bit of a bad reputation, and people often stand clear of them. The good news is that they don't have to be a lot of work. In this chapter I'd like to show you how you can bring freedom and joy into your homeschool by sharing some valuable information and tips which I have gained and used over the past twenty years of teaching my eight children at home.

## Our Testimonials and Experiences with Unit Studies

Our children truly have a love for books and learning, but this happened quite by accident. Let me explain! When we started homeschooling, we used traditional methods for at least the first four years because that's what was available. Soon I found myself with three grumbling school-age children who each had a foot-high stack of textbooks, accompanied by my own foot-high stack of teacher's manuals—for each child! My children did everything they could to avoid having to do school. In desperation I realized I must do something different so I tried a unit study. My basic understanding was that a unit study was a teaching method where you chose a topic and tried to fit your academic subjects into it. When I announced to my children, "Guys, we are going to do something different today," there was a unanimous shout of, "Yahoo!" Our first study was on trains, and my children responded with much enthusiasm and even started asking: "When are we going to get started? What are we going to do today? What are we going to study next?" Well, I didn't know exactly what I was going to do next, but I did know I was not going to go back into the bondage I had experienced using textbooks.

We have used the unit study method exclusively ever since, bumbling our way across the years. In the process we have discovered some simple principles and guidelines that help make this method doable for all. I feel that I have sort of "worked the bugs out of unit studies," and while many people approach this method differently, I would like to show you what we do and what has worked for us for many years. I think you'll find it user-friendly and exciting!

OK, I can read your mind. You're thinking, *Sure, Jennifer does unit studies as a means of survival because she has so many children!* Truly, that is one reason we started with unit studies, but this method became the vehicle we used to bring delight to our studies. How can you tell children love to learn? They love to talk about things they've learned, and you can see a spark of enthusiasm in their faces. They may even verbalize this by telling you they love school! One Mother's Day my husband asked the children to all say something they appreciated about me. They each had some nice things to say, but most of them commented that they liked the way I teach. This indeed was heartwarming, but I knew they meant they enjoyed our style of learning. This was like getting a huge paycheck and also a positive indicator that this method works! I've also noticed a spirit of cooperation: my children don't fight me anymore and usually look forward to the next topic/study. You might think your children would never say they love school, or you might think your children wouldn't cooperate, but I have taught hundreds of parents how to use unit studies applying these principles, and many come and share their success stories with me, telling how much their homeschools have changed and how using this method has brought joy into their teaching.

## Why This Method Works

This method appeals to so many learning styles, which encourages and fosters true learning and delight; and when your children are delighting in learning, it is such a joy to the teacher. My fifteen-year-old daughter, Brooke, had a recent conversation with some girls her age. She was wide-eyed and excited as she discussed great literature and favorite authors with the girls. Indifferent, another girl said, "I'd never read a book twice unless it was assigned." Later the other girls told my daughter she was the smartest girl they had ever met. Now, I think Brooke is pretty sharp, but I wouldn't classify her as a genius. (Sorry, Brookie!)

What these girls observed was that Brooke enjoys talking about books and learning. You can't force children to be delighted, but you must lead them into an environment where it can be fostered. Often kids who just go through the motions, checking off the required boxes, miss out on the joy of learning and only get an education because they have to, not because they are fascinated by learning about God's world and can see how exciting and valuable a true education can be.

I went through school getting mostly As, but I did not get an education. I achieved good grades simply by doing my assigned work. I was not a reader, so I was left out of literary circles. Friends called me "Miss Brainy," but I knew I was not smart. Please listen moms—we have the opportunity to provide a real education for our children, so let us not make the mistake of jumping through academic hoops and reacting by fearing that we might miss something important. Remember, even though information is contained in a textbook, if it is dry and boring, your children will miss it. I have asked students questions about history, for instance, and they can't answer. The information went in but did not get digested; they only did what was required to make the grade. On the flip side, when your children do a unit study, they become somewhat of an expert on many topics and retain what they learned much better because it was interesting to them, and they made use of many of their senses during the study, and they enjoyed learning about it. So be assured that you always do a more thorough job with a unit study!

This method can be a lifesaver for those who are teaching multilevel because all students study the same topic, each working at his or her own skill and ability level. I emphasize that this method is a wonderful approach whether you are teaching one child or many. In addition, by combining students together, you not only save time (and sanity for mom!), but it also promotes unity because everyone learns the same material, and then rich discussions take place even in "nonschool" times and further learning occurs, sometimes simply because of the reviewing that is going on.

Some of the characteristics of the unit study method include being more hands-on, interactive, mind engaging, and more relaxed—using a living books- /literature-based approach. It was a surprise to me that some mistakenly think this method is an academically inferior approach suitable for lazy people who like to do crafts! Let me assure you that this is not the case—at least not with the folks I encounter who use the unit study approach and who follow the guidelines I encourage and teach.

## Jumping into How to Do a Unit Study

Way back when I started teaching via unit study, I read a book about unit studies. I got so excited I could hardly keep from jumping for joy. Although I was convinced this was the way to go, I still didn't have any idea what to actually do. Over the years I have discovered what I call problem areas with unit studies, and I offer some specific guidelines in what we'll call "The Steward Method."

### THERE ARE NO RULES

People often say, "I don't think I'm doing it right." Enjoy the freedom in knowing there is no absolutely correct way to do a unit study. Just think in terms of learning all about something, approach it from different angles, incorporate many of the child's senses, and you have a unit study! If you want to study frogs with your preschooler, plan on reading some books and stories about frogs, collect some pollywogs from a pond, draw a picture, name five types of frogs, play leapfrog, work on recognizing and writing the letter *F* for frog, and you have a unit study!

Another important factor to remember is that you are not trying to learn *everything* there is to know about the topic but rather to become familiar with it. Here's my little secret: your goal as the teacher is to slip in as many academic subjects as possible, which in turn offers you an avenue to continue to build skills. If you were to study pioneers and read a book on the Oregon Trail, afterwards would be a perfect time to use a black line map and mark the trail, forts along the way, landmarks, and such. During this activity your children enjoy learning and don't even realize they just covered geography. Their completed work should go into their notebook section labeled "Geography and Diagrams."

### Relax

Next you need to relax and trust. You cannot force this love for learning; it takes time and needs to be fostered in a relaxed environment. Get rid of your long list of "what ifs" and don't be afraid. The Lord is behind your homeschooling efforts, and he happens to know your children and their needs better than you! So, if you catch yourself saying, "I'm afraid of . . .," this is not from the Lord. We do not want to have a fear-based approach to our teaching! Many parents are deeply concerned about college when their oldest child is only three years old!

## Guiding Principles

With these things in mind, now we can proceed into some of the principles we teach in The Steward Method.[1]

I refer to this as "The Prescription Framework," which provides something concrete to adhere to, while still being able to maintain a relaxed atmosphere. I floundered until I discovered this framework because I had nothing to go by. This framework consists of the things we do the same with each study, so I always know what to do, and my children know what to expect. We just change the topic and slide the new books and topic into the framework. Whether you use a complete unit study curriculum, a topical guide, or design your own studies, you can have success by using this prescription framework!

## TIME FRAME

We recommend taking one month for each topic/study. This is just a guideline (some studies take more or less time), but it seems to be the right amount of time to cover the material and adequately learn about the topic without losing the interest of the student. You could study some topics all year because there is so much to learn, but the children would grow weary of the topic.

## BUILDING NOTEBOOKS

Each of our children builds a notebook as a project, using one-inch, view-front, three-ringed binders. Divide your notebook into sections for each subject and encourage creativity, so this project actually becomes a report! My kids love their notebooks and enjoy collecting postcards, photos, stickers, and other items as they are learning, which enhance their notebooks.[2]

## ASSIGNMENT SHEET

I try to write up an assignment sheet (early in the study) with check-off boxes so my older children can be more self-directed. This is a list of activities (arranged by subjects) they can do in different subject areas without me.

## Daily Schedule

I'm not generally a scheduled person because something is always coming up, but working with a daily schedule for our studies has been a key to our success. It works like this: 9:00–12:00: Bible, reading aloud, information time, then lunch. My children have their basics, which include: reading (one hour a day broken into two thirty-minute sessions), their phonics workbook, and math. If I am not ready to start our study, they know they need to do their basics. Also, almost every day they work on an assignment from their assignment sheet (after lunch), and we usually do some activity together, which falls into some subject area, after information time. I find if I give my children these three hours things go so well the rest of the day and we get so much done. By the end of the study, my children have a notebook filled with their work, which is the result of learning. Imagine having six or more notebooks each year for each child! What a feeling of accomplishment. Plus, I save time this way. If they haven't already done their basics, they will do them in the afternoon, but they are usually done with everything by around 2:00 or so.

## Reading Aloud

We consider read-aloud time to be the most important subject after Bible time because of the content of the story and the discussion that ensues. There are so many benefits to reading aloud we cannot begin to list them, but perhaps the biggest is the atmosphere that is fostered; this is where you truly develop a love for learning, so make sure you make it a priority. Reading aloud and spending this awesome time together accomplishes the biggest strides toward developing a love for learning. But you must relax and let it happen over time! It's what you take the time to do—not what you say—that demonstrates your priorities and makes the most difference. Reading aloud equals delight in learning from literature or stories.

## INFORMATION TIME

This is where I read from nonfiction books. Much instruction and learning take place during this time. You can gather your kids close and show them pictures and diagrams, and usually you can do some connecting activity (in some subject), which is a result of something learned. Information time equals learning from nonfiction books.

## THE BOOKS

It's really the books that make the study. Get all kinds of different books on your topic. If you're studying medieval times, why not get a book on how to play chess? Others would include picture storybooks for young children, novels at the child's level for independent reading, educational coloring books, nonfiction books, cookbooks, and the like. A good rule of thumb is to get around ten books. I find it hard to stay within that number, but if you get too many books, you can't remember which book had that map or information you spotted during your planning time.

## SUBJECTS

With conventional methods, some folks spend an hour a day for each subject and don't have the time or energy to get to the unit study, so in The Steward Method we suggest including as many subjects as possible. For subjects that need a little more of the mechanics taught, like spelling and grammar, spend an hour or so a week instead of an hour a day. Subjects that fit well are: history, science, geography, most language arts (spelling, vocabulary, reading, writing, and handwriting), art, and music. The subjects that we leave out are math, Bible, and phonics. There's one more important thing about subjects. Ready? Teach history or science, not both in the same unit. If you are doing a unit study on the Civil War, just let it be history. The next month you can do a science topic like weather, and instead of trying to figure out how to fit history into it by researching famous meteorologists throughout history or when specific floods happened, you can just let the study of weather be a science topic. This really makes more sense to the students and makes planning so much easier for you!

Keep the vision and remember the big picture of why God has called you to homeschool your children. What does he want to accomplish in and through their lives? We are given the privilege to teach them at home, the best place to impress God's ways on their hearts. If you are able to succeed in your teaching, not just academics but in building godly character and valuable life skills, just imagine a mighty kingdom of warriors coming up in the next generations! This chapter cannot cover everything, but hopefully we have offered some insight into how wonderful this method of teaching can be and given you some ideas for how to carry them out. Now go get started on your first unit study! The sky is the limit!

## Endnotes

1. Jennifer Steward, *Everything You Need to Know about Homeschool Unit Studies* (Steward Ship, 1999).
2. Jennifer Steward, *Everything You Need to Build a Unit Study Notebook* (Steward Ship).

＊  ＊  ＊

The Stewards have been homeschooling their eight children from their Northern California home for twenty years. Jennifer has gained much experience using unit studies with her children and is considered an expert. Their home business, Steward Ship, began with the development of the The Choreganizer chore system. They also provide curriculum and support materials for the unit study method.

The Stewards travel about offering different workshops. Jennifer has taught hundreds of parents how to use this method and is also a popular speaker at homeschool conventions bringing insight and humor from her experiences. Request a free catalog: 888-4 R UNITS (888-478-6487) or visit their Web site at www.unitstudies.com.

# Special
# Needs Unit

* * * * * * * * * * * * * * * * * * * *

*There is gold, and a multitude of rubies;*
*but the lips of knowledge are a precious jewel.*

—PROVERBS 20:15

❋ ❋ ❋

*Teaching should be such that what is offered is*
*perceived as a valuable gift and not a hard duty.*

—ALBERT EINSTEIN

As homeschooling has once again become an acceptable education track for families, the number of parents choosing to bring home their students with special educational needs has grown. An estimated six million students in the United States alone are considered to have disabilities, and another three million are considered gifted students. The parents of these students seek answers, share information, provide support to others, share the joy of little accomplishments, and offer a shoulder during the trials of life with a child who has challenges.

Some parents choose to homeschool their special needs children due to dissatisfaction with the services provided by teachers in the public school system. Others had already planned to homeschool and have just received a diagnosis or explanation of why a child has certain habits or developmental restraints; they choose to continue their homeschool journey. While some children with special needs are effectively mainstreamed in the school system, others don't fare so well. Being at home provides them with a safe place to learn and grow, free from the risk of being forgotten or left behind as the rest of the class moves on through their lessons. On the other side of the coin, gifted students are able to fast-forward through lessons at their own speed and can face intellectual challenges catered to their interests and ability levels. Students with great talent in fields such as art or music may find much more freedom to pursue their God-given talent without having to sacrifice as much on the general core of their education.

No matter what a family's reasons for keeping a special needs child home, or bringing them home from the public education system, the most important thing is that they are out there! Special needs families are a growing population within the homeschool community. While they may seek support from organizations and companies that cater to a child's specific needs, they also need the assistance of those who are most familiar with their general education methods. Here to describe their families' journeys of homeschooling special needs students are Sherry Bushnell, of the organization NATHHAN, and Christine M. Field, author of *Homeschooling the Challenging Child*. As you will learn from our authors, no two children with special education needs are the same; nor are their families. There are a variety of options available to every special educator, including homeschoolers, and the overwhelming message these ladies share with us is, "It can be done!"

# Special Needs

## Christine M. Field

Special needs. The label refers to a child, but the sentiment should more accurately be applied to the parents of challenging children. We have special needs as well. We need information, expertise, encouragement, support, materials, and sometimes help!

Do you have a special needs child? The label can be Down's syndrome, Asperger's, ADHD, learning disabled, or something else. Each presents unique challenges.

You are a special parent with a special child. Let me assure you that you *can* homeschool that child. You don't have to completely turn your life over to the experts although you might choose to partner with them at some point in your child's educational program.

Did your special child come to you at birth with a physical challenge? Or did you discover that uniqueness later as gifts and talents began to unfold?

Our introduction to special needs came with the third of our four children. We were feeling pretty good about being homeschooling parents. The oldest two were quick learners and a delight to teach. The third one was a challenge. Despite two years of intensive phonics instruction, she couldn't read. She laboriously sounded out each letter, often mistaking one for another. By the time she reached the end of a sentence, she was so exhausted from her effort that she did not remember the point of the passage. Her memory was extremely challenged, and she was highly distractible, often complaining that noises and her own bodily sensations kept her from concentrating. After the success we attained in teaching the oldest two, this child left me feeling like an utter failure as a teacher and as a mother.

We started piecing the puzzle together, beginning with our own observations. We did a tremendous amount of research on learning disabilities and attention deficit disorder. And we prayed long and hard for this puzzling child.

As she was nearing the end of her second-grade year of homeschooling, we contacted our local school district to ask for their input. Under Illinois law, where I live, a parent can raise the issue of a learning disability to the school district. When the issue is raised, they are required to do an evaluation. Opinions differ as to the wisdom of this practice. The Home School Legal Defense Association (HSLDA) is against any type of public school intervention. Private evaluators are available to assess children, but they can be costly for many parents. We felt confident because we knew many of the professionals in our school district. We also took her for a complete medical and optical screening and sought an extensive evaluation by a private child psychologist for ADHD.

Ultimately, she was deemed to be a fairly routine case of both LD (Learning Disabled) and ADD (Attention Deficit Disorder). While she may have been routine for the examiners, the discovery of her challenges rocked our homeschool to its foundation! Although she did not exhibit the hyperactive component of ADD, we learned that an equally powerful spectrum of the disorder is characterized by inattentiveness, moodiness, and lower energy behavior.

With lots of hard work and research, in consultation with a reading specialist at our local school, she is now doing well. Just last week we learned that she was reading at grade level! We are giving God the glory for her progress. She still struggles with spelling, written expression, and math, and may do so for the rest of her life, but I am confident she is being well equipped.

This was our path. It may or may not be yours. The goal of this chapter is to encourage you that you do have options in education for your special needs child whether that need is relatively mild or all encompassing.

When people learn that we homeschool a special needs child, they generally have five questions. This chapter will seek to answer them. They are:

1. Is it legal to homeschool a special needs child?
2. Is it best for the child?
3. Will the child be OK?
4. Can I handle it?
5. How do I get started?

## 1. Is It Legal?

The First and Fourteenth Amendments of the Constitution protect your right to homeschool your child. You have the same legal right to homeschool your special needs child as you do any other child. Certain states may require more accountability from you. Their regulations may be more stringent. You should research your state law thoroughly before you begin. Check your state's requirements by contacting your local state or county board of education or the Home School Legal Defense Association (www.hslda.org).

While you are empowered by the United States Constitution to homeschool, you may be subject to subtle or overt pressure to enroll your child in school. This is especially the case if you are receiving special services from your local school. It is always within your control to say a polite "No thank you" to school officials who would seek to have you send your child to school full-time. In my situation we have been able to work out an extremely productive arrangement for tutoring that has been an enormous blessing for us. Many parents use public services for things like speech therapy and physical therapy and then pursue their own educational program at home. They are able to take advantage of the expertise of the school district while maintaining their family's home training and discipleship program.

## 2. Is It Best?

The world will focus on your child's differences rather than their strengths. Children who learn, look, or act differently may experience self-confidence and self-esteem issues as they interact in the world. By choosing to provide some or all of your child's education at home, you are giving them a tender shelter under which to flourish. If your child is already in school in a special education system, bringing them home may bring healing for emotions damaged by the negativity of that situation. Teaching our special children at home spares them the brunt of comparison and competition that are rampant in the classroom. It also allows us to help them nurture friendships that are God honoring and respecting of individual differences, apart from the pain and ridicule of school.

Another reason homeschooling your special child might be best is the tremendous benefit of flexibility. In your program you can strengthen your child's weaknesses and teach to their strengths. You can use materials on many grade levels depending on your child's needs. (You can even abandon the concept of "grade level" altogether and just teach!) By homeschooling your special child, there is no stigma or shame. Rather than using the most popular curriculum at the moment, you can use materials and instruction that are appropriate for that individual child. It is a custom education.

You can also exercise greater control over your child's physical environment. Does your child have special dietary needs? Your program won't be sabotaged by bad food or a negative environment.

Perhaps most importantly, homeschooling can afford you the opportunity to impart God-honoring values and to build on your family's strengths. You can be instrumental in instilling in your child that he is a person of value and worth.

Tom and Sherry Bushnell of the National Challenged Homeschoolers Associated Network (NATHHAN) are the true pioneers and heroes of teaching special needs children at home. In their book, *Christian Homes and Special Kids* they describe their feelings about whether this path is best. They write that the parents of special needs kids are

> trapped between a rock and a hard place. We are
> Christian families dealing with disability. We are con-
> cerned about a godly education for our children with
> special needs. For many of us, choosing to carefully edu-
> cate our children with special needs at home is fun.
> Fun? Yes, we count the time invested in the lives of our
> special needs children a well-thought-out investment in
> the future. How many of us want to spend the rest of
> our lives with an ill-mannered, selfish, skill-less,
> unhappy, disabled adult? Not us! We may have been
> given a different role in life as a parent of a child with
> special needs, but we are not going to be miserable in
> our golden years.[1]

It may be difficult to look beyond the challenge of raising and teaching a special needs child. But I want to encourage you to look to the future at the person you will launch into adulthood. This is where you can catch your vision for homeschooling! Setting that long-range goal will help you make the shorter term decisions about your child's education and character development.

## 3. Will They Be OK?

I have learned that doubt (and often discouragement) is a predictable part of the homeschooling journey. I experience doubt even while homeschooling my "normal" kids. How do we know any of them will be OK? The stunning academic success of homeschooled kids has been well documented.[2] How about the rest of our kids?

One academic study set out to determine if ordinary parents, not certified teachers, could provide an adequate learning environment for special needs kids. Using only a small sample of students, the study looked at the amount of time students spent making academic responses. "Academic responses" means the amount of time spent responding to mom's teaching. In educational circles the amount of time a child is engaged with the teacher is called academic engaged time (AET). Generally an increase in academic engaged time (AET) will lead to an increase in achievement gains. This academic study showed that "generally, the measures of classroom ecology and achievement showed that home schools, when compared to special education programs, provided equal if not more advantageous instructional environments for children with learning disabilities." Because there are fewer children in the home, they enjoy greater academic engaged time (AET). They also gained more, overall, on standardized testing. The study's authors noted, "Ten times as much one-on-one instruction was observed in home school versus public school settings." The testing showed homeschooled students making large gains in reading and written language while the public school students lost ground in reading and made only small gains in written language.[3]

We know that we can accomplish more in a few hours of intense instruction than a classroom teacher with twenty or thirty students can accomplish in six hours of the school day. Because of this increased one-on-one time, homeschooling has been referred to as the Cadillac of education. When we learn the skills and techniques to meet the needs of our special children, our time with them can be focused and productive. We can rest assured they will be OK, however God defines that for each individual child. Your special needs child can have that same experience.

## 4. Can I Do It?

It is only after walking through many challenges in my life that I can affirm without a doubt that God uses our weaknesses. Moses felt inadequate. He complained to God,

> "O Lord, I have never been eloquent, neither in the past nor since you have spoken to your servant. I am slow of speech and tongue. The Lord said to him, 'Who gave man his mouth? Who makes him deaf or mute? Who gives him sight or makes him blind? Is it not I, the LORD? Now go; I will help you speak and will teach you what to say.'" (Exod. 4:10–12 NIV)

Moses hesitated and doubted himself, yet God used him mightily. God can use you mightily to make a difference in your child's life, no matter how inadequate you may feel. God spoke to the apostle Paul and said, "My grace is sufficient for you, for my power is made perfect in weakness" (2 Cor. 12:9 NIV).

Let God work through your weaknesses. In his grace he can accomplish what he wishes in your life and in your child's life. When we lay our burdens and the tasks that seem insurmountable at his feet, he opens doors of opportunity and brings encouragers alongside as we navigate the path ahead.

## 5. How Do I Get Started?

I remember being a beginner homeschooler. I felt overwhelmed! I was obsessed with answering the questions of what to do, how to do it, when to do it, and more. I felt I would never get the hang of it.

I still have days where I doubt, but the overarching comfort is the knowledge that I am doing what I believe God has called me to do and I am doing what I believe is best for my children. While facing these getting-started jitters, keep these priorities in clear view while making the other decisions, and God will help you to make them wisely.

There is no one way to homeschool, and there is no one way to homeschool a challenging child. I found this frustrating upon learning of my daughter's diagnosis because I wanted someone to give me all the answers and how-tos. But the journey of arriving at our own customized solutions has been a wonderful learning process for all of us.

The following are a few approaches to planning your child's program.

### PLANNING A PROGRAM

1. You can partner with your local public school although you should be forewarned that this is a matter of some controversy within the homeschooling community. Some would advise you not to allow this government intrusion in your home. I am adamantly opposed to allowing greater government control over

our homes, yet where does that leave the parent who truly needs help but cannot afford to secure all services on a private basis? Don't condemn these partnerships without investigating them first. You must do what is in your child's best interest.

2. You can work with a consultant on a private basis. The Home School Legal Defense Association (HSLDA) offers a special needs consultant. Almaden Valley Christian School, led by special needs author and consultant Sharon Hensley, can help you design a complete program. Christian Cottage Schools with Mike and Teri Spray are available to help you plan your program. Dr. Joe Sutton of Exceptional Diagnostics offers testing and curriculum consultation. Contact information for each of these is in the resource section at the end of this chapter. Their fees vary greatly as well as the level of services they offer. Many more consultants are available, but these are ones I have had personal contact and experience with. If you live near a university or medical school, some offer clinics where graduate students are learning to be therapists can provide services at great savings.

3. You can design your own exclusive program by becoming an expert on your child's challenge and designing your own therapies and approaches. The downside to this approach is that you will need to give yourself time to educate yourself and get up to speed on your child's limitations and the best practices for dealing with it.

*If you have chosen to get a professional diagnosis, what should you do next?*

Start with your family physician or pediatrician. Let him rule out any organic reasons for your difficulties. He can also be a good source for referrals to other professionals.

The Internet is a great tool for researching your specific issues, as it will allow you to gather a great deal of information quickly. Take care to check the reliability of that information. Some well-established sites, such as the National Center for

Learning Disabilities, at www.ncld.org, are a great starting point for your research.

If you choose to work with more than one professional, make sure they are all communicating with one another. A teamwork approach is needed, with the parents working as the day-to-day coaches.

If you have decided to approach your public school for a learning disability evaluation, how do you find out if your child is eligible for special education? Rather than a casual phone call, send a written request to the director of special education or the principal of your child's school. In your letter express your concern and give some reasons you think your child has a disability and needs special education help. Ask the school to evaluate your child as soon as practical.

They may agree to an evaluation or they may not. If they do agree, the school must evaluate your child at no cost to you within sixty days of their consent. Be advised that the school does not have to evaluate your child just because you have asked. If the school refuses to evaluate your child, they must let you know this decision in writing along with the reasons for their refusal. Along with their communications with you, they should have furnished to you a document that delineates your rights to an appeal from their decision. If you choose to challenge their decision, you follow the procedure prescribed.

*How is an assessment done?*

For a learning disability, the assessment involves several components:

- An assessment of intellectual potential or IQ, such as the Stanford-Binet Intelligence Scale or the Woodcock-Johnson Pyscho-Educational Battery

- An assessment of the child's information processing or motor ability—to isolate whether the learning difficulty is in the visual, auditory, or motor system
- An assessment of current educational achievement (grade level), such as the Wechsler Individual Achievement Test or the Wide Range Achievement Test

An evaluation for ADHD usually involves:

- An extensive developmental history
- Detailed questionnaires to the student (if older), his parents and teachers—One of the most common tests is called the Conners' Parent Rating Scale, developed by C. Keith Conners, PhD. It asks the evaluator to look at eighty categories of behavior and rate whether the behavior is never present, seldom present, often present, or very often present.
- Other tests at the discretion of the psychologist—Some are using a computer-based program that measures a child's ability to attend or tendency to act impulsively. This is not yet standard practice, and your professional may or may not offer this assessment.

How can you prepare your child for this experience? We prepared our daughter by telling her she was going to go play some games with some nice people. Although she is a bit shy, she adapted to the situation quite well. We did not tell her too far in advance because she would have fretted for an unnecessarily long time. We told her just beforehand and answered all her questions about the process.

If you choose to have your child evaluated by the school district, consult *The Parents' Complete Special Education Guide*, full of sample letters, checklists, and more.[4]

BEFORE YOU SIGN ON THE DOTTED LINE

Parents, especially parents with challenging children, can be the target of a seller's market. Whether you are looking for curriculum or special therapy programs, look closely before investing your child's future or your money. Anyone can write a program and sell it. Some are good and some are useless. Here are some tough questions to ask:

*Is this approach/therapy based on scientific research?*

This means it was tested on a large sample so results can be generalized to other people. It wasn't just used with the author's three children who did beautifully, so your child will too. It also means the researchers were objective. They weren't affiliated with any company that might benefit from their results. In true scientific research, procedures are compared with a control group, which is a group that did not receive the therapy or program. Finally, the results were measured statistically so the relationships between the numbers can be seen.

*How long has the company or supplier existed?*

This is not to say that a new, groundbreaking approach doesn't exist, but the longer something has been working, the greater likelihood it will work for you.

*Especially if you are expending large sums of cash, is there any guarantee?*

What are the financial implications or penalties of opting out of the program?

When your child is suffering or has a significant problem, it can make you feel desperate to get help. Your child needs your calm, well-thought-out response to the situation. Pray hard, talk it out, and educate yourself before making decisions.

## Homeschool IEPs

"What does your child's IEP say?" is a question you are likely to hear among special needs circles. It stands for Individualized Education Program and refers to the formal plan a public school is required by law to draft once there has been a diagnosis of a disability.

Although an IEP is not usually formally necessary when homeschooling a special needs child, giving some thought to the components of an IEP can be helpful, especially when you design your own curriculum. Seeing a written plan and set of goals in place helps keep you on track for the year. It also provides you with documentation of your homeschooling activity in the unlikely event that your homeschooling is called into question. Whether we label them as an IEP or not, it is a plan for your homeschooling. If you don't have a goal and a purpose for your instruction, you won't know whether you have been successful.

Your IEP should include the following components:

1. Document and comment on your child's current ability level. Note how she is doing now in the areas of math, reading, written and oral expression. This can be a formal assessment or samples of his work.
2. Make yearly and short-term (quarterly) goals for each area of weakness. What do you want your child to learn this year or this month? Make these goals short and specific. For example, for the first quarter of the year, your goal might be to recognize the beginning sounds of five consonants: *b*, *c*, *m*, *l*, and *p*. This gives a focus to your work and a way to know if you have met the mark.
3. Note what materials and methods you will use. List the books, materials, or special services you are using.
4. Finally, evaluate how it's going. Once a quarter evaluate your progress toward the short-term goals listed. This

can be an anecdotal narrative or a formal assessment. It's the answer to the question, How's it going?

How do you find out appropriate goals for your child in his or her unique situation? Several publications can assist you:

- NATHHAN, the premier source for information on home-schooling special needs children, publishes a book called *Individual Education Planning Manual for the Homeschool Handicapped Student* by Deborah Mary Kathleen Mills. Contact www.nathhan.org.
- *Practical Guide to Writing Goals and Objectives* by Steenburgen, Geib, and Steenburgen-Geib, available through Academic Therapy Publications, 1981.
- *Skills Evaluation for the Home School* by Rebecca Avery, and may be ordered through Alpha Omega Publications, www.aop.com.

Sometimes progress is obvious and big. Often it is small and incremental. Sharon Hensley from Almaden Valley Christian School puts it this way:

> For the majority of families, progress is NOT the big "send off the fireworks" kind of stuff, but the small, daily-grind type of progress that is often harder to see. I encourage my families to think of progress as small steps forward from where ever their child is now—not as "how close to normal" are they. I think homeschool families with special needs kids often feel discouraged and defeated because they don't give themselves credit for the small daily progresses, like a child attending for 10 minutes instead of only 5 minutes, or a student working 10 math problems all in the right direction![5]

Delighting in the small steps instead of despairing over the big picture is the way to keep being enthusiastic and encouraged.

## The Very Young Child

Sometimes we are concerned with the development of a young, preschool age child. Consultation with your pediatrician is your first responsibility. Your doctor can compare growth patterns against proven normative charts and tell you appropriate milestones for each age of development. The best thing you can do for younger children (prior to school age) is to get a listing of those developmental milestones and work on those as a goal list with your child in close consultation with your physician. Even if he seems "far behind," just work through the skills in order and honor your child's timetable. These lists of milestones are available everywhere—from your pediatrician for free—but there are also books showing the steps of development. One that we used when the children were young was *Slow and Steady, Get Me Ready* by June Oberland. It gives day-by-day activities to do with your child from birth to age five. Although we did not slavishly do every single exercise, it was comforting to know that we were tracking appropriate skill milestones.

Joyce Herzog has also written two neat volumes: *Luke's School List* and *Luke's Life List* (www.JoyceHerzog.com). One lists incremental steps of development in academic skills and the other in life skills. If you are preparing your own program, these books can be helpful.

## General Principles

You should have settled a few bottom-line priorities in your heart before you begin your program of homeschooling your special needs child.

*You must have settled in your heart the answer to the question, Why are we homeschooling?*

The days will come when you doubt your decision, and so your convictions should be firm. You should also be in complete agreement with your spouse. If either of you is against the idea, the stresses left on the other spouse to go it alone will be overwhelming. The Bible says a house divided cannot stand. The same is true for a homeschool.

*Your child must know what is expected of him in all arenas of life.* That means behavior, work habits, chores, and more. It is important to send a clear, positive message that putting forth his best effort is the only acceptable option. Bring him on board as your partner in learning and respect his input, whenever reasonable.

*Remember that repetition and routine create good habits—both for our children and us!*

*Begin with realistic, bottom-line priorities for your child.*

It is unrealistic to expect your child to become fluent in Latin in one semester. It is realistic that he will learn to count from one to twenty-five. Write down your goals for the child, being as specific as possible. This is your Individualized Educational Program at its essence.

*Don't overreact to your child's difficulties by excessive displays of sympathy or sadness.*

Children can be tremendously sensitive to your feelings, and such overreaction will only make them feel worse. You may be sad and frustrated, but your child is undoubtedly feeling the same emotions. He needs you to be the adult and in control of your feelings and help him learn to control his.

*Say and think positive things about your child.*

When your child hears you talking to others within their earshot, it is powerful medicine. A mention to grandma, such as, "Johnny did an awesome job writing the letter *A* today," will build his self-esteem and confidence. As a labeled child, he may feel that he is damaged somehow, so he must experience success to begin to unlearn a failure syndrome.

*Point out the relationship between effort and improvement.*

Prove to them that they *can* learn. By experiencing small successes, they begin to see that there is a correlation between trying hard and being successful

*Establish control in your house.*

Life with a challenging child can feel out of control. Make sure your discipline and boundaries are clear and consistent.

*Give the child small choices.*

Would they rather do math or reading first? Would they like the yellow pencil or the green pencil? This helps them to feel a sense of control and will lead to greater cooperation in more difficult matters.

*Be sure to relate new information to already known information.*

When studying fractions, talk about pizza! What is in your environment that you can relate to the concept being studied?

*Abandon the concept of grade level.*

Your child is at *his* level, and that's where he is! Organizing children into grade levels is how schools manage large groups of children. You are not a school. You are nurturing your child.

*Focus on your goal: a godly, functioning child.*

Since I am responsible for how this child is launched into the world, I would rather have them be spiritually grounded, wholesome, respectful and polite than be a Latin scholar.

## CHOOSING CURRICULUM

I have fantasized about going to the learning disabilities catalog and ordering the complete third-grade curriculum, but guess what? It doesn't exist. Most of us end up pulling our curriculum from a variety of sources. Your child might need one approach in math and another approach to phonics. In general no one supplier can provide all you need.

Even when using a variety of suppliers, you will likely have to modify whatever you choose. As an example, picture the learning-disabled child with an attention problem. His mother sits him at the kitchen table with a worksheet containing thirty problems. The pages are colorful and attractive. But this visual overload is almost overwhelming for this child. The problems are closely spaced with insufficient room to perform calculations, as this child's handwriting is large. This single page can absolutely paralyze a child!

A better initial choice might be to choose a workbook with less color. You can also construct a viewing box out of poster board consisting of a small viewing window placed over the current problem. Doing this serves to block out the other work and allows the child to focus on one problem at a time. You might also cut out one row for him to do, thereby reducing the number of problems. Small numbers can be enlarged on a copier. These modifications can take a workbook for a standard curriculum and transform it into something with which a challenged child can experience success.

When you choose your materials, don't neglect other factors such as your teaching style, your budget, the other children in the family, and the time required to work with the challenged child. Many parents of challenging children feel that 20 percent of their family receives 80 percent of their energy and attention. Can you make modifications to share the teaching time required? In our home we have the older children take turns doing drills and computer work with the younger children. We even used this as an opportunity for them to earn extra money. For each computer therapy session they completed, they were paid one dollar or earned points toward a trip to the candy store.

Be realistic about the time you have available to make or use a lot of extraneous materials. It may be your heart's desire to make learning games, charts, and other reinforcing materials, but it might save your sanity to take a trip to the teacher's store to purchase these items rather than trying to find the time to construct them from scratch.

If all of your child's day is spent working on problem areas, she will learn to dread school time. The goal of your program should be to create a balance each day of things she feels good about and things she struggles with. In our home, math and phonics are the most tedious and time-consuming. Therefore, I make certain that history, geography, science, Bible, and the arts are hands-on, project oriented, and as much fun as I can squeeze out of them. The children are assured that if they get through the hard stuff they will be able to use their considerable strengths in the other subject areas.

How would this work? It is limited only by your imagination. We recently toured through ancient history (again). While my daughter had considerable difficulty with the minimal assigned reading, she loved watching a video, building a pyramid, doing pop-up books, working with clay to carve hieroglyphics, and using Sculpey to make tomb artifacts. These did not require her to focus on her weakness—reading—but allowed her to experience success. This encouraged her to read the two readers she was assigned to read independently, and the unit was satisfying and rewarding. She is able to retell volumes of stories about the time period studied—far more than if I had merely required her to read out of a book.

So what's so hard about that? It's the 80/20 principle again, this time in reverse. Because of your child's challenges, the hard stuff, which might normally take up 20 percent of your time and energy, will take up 80 percent of it.

The learning experts refer to this as making sure your instruction has a balance of remediation and compensation. Remediation means going to the core of the issue and working directly on the weaknesses and is most appropriate for the younger child or the child with less severe problems. Compensation means teaching strategies for dealing with the issues and is more appropriate for older children or those with severe problems. Keep in mind that the older your student, the more he will need to focus on content areas, like history and science, to prepare him to deal with upper level courses.

For the younger child, if this makes you feel overwhelmed by your teaching and preparation load, focus on the basics and pick fewer skills to work on at a time. Then add in the things like science and history, the content area of which will be repeated multiple times throughout the school years. Look at any sample scope and sequence and see how many times plants, for example, are studied from kindergarten through twelfth grade. The amount of repetition, with ever-increasing complexity, is staggering. If you do not thoroughly cover a content area, rest assured your child will revisit it at some time in his academic career.

## DOING THE HARD THINGS

Nothing worthwhile was ever accomplished in my life without struggle. I sought easy answers to the challenges posed by my daughter but discovered there was no easy path. My choice was this: Give the challenge over to the school system or educate myself and stay spiritually connected enough to meet the challenge. I chose the latter path. The journey is hard, but God is faithful. When my child reaches maturity, I will be able to say with confidence that I did all I could possibly do to help her.

No regrets.
> *Let us not become weary in doing good,*
> *for at the proper time we will reap a harvest*
> *if we do not give up.*

—GALATIANS 6:9 NIV

## Getting Started: General Resources

NATHHAN/CHASK
PO Box 39
Porthill, ID 83853
208-267-6246
www.chask.org
www.nathhan.com

This is the place to start for any type of learning issues. The Web site is a virtual education in special needs. They have a newsletter, lending library, and helpful Web forums.

Home School Legal Defense Association (HSLDA)
PO Box 3000
Purcellville, VA 20134
540-338-5600
www.hslda.org

Contact them to learn the homeschooling law in your state. Ask for their booklet on homeschooling special needs children.

PROGRAM PLANNING/TESTING/CURRICULUM CONSULTING

Sharon Hensley, M.A.
Almaden Valley Christian School
6291 Vegas Drive
San Jose, CA 95120
408-997-0290
www.almadenvalleychristianschool.com

Author of *Home Schooling Children with Special Needs.* Provides curriculum development and support to enrolled families. She has a Special Needs Home School Starter Kit that is incredibly helpful. We devoured the kit, beginning with the book, *Home Schooling Children with Special Needs,* which teaches us first to distinguish between learning differences and learning difficulties. The book thoroughly explains each and also explores other disabilities, gives specific instruction for planning a homeschool program and offers encouragement for dealing with the many emotional issues involved in raising these children. Mrs. Hensley brings warmth and encouragement to her work, and her knowledge is from her formal education (M.A. in special education) and life experience (homeschooling mom of three children, one with autism).

After devouring the book, I listened to her audiotapes, *Understanding and Teaching Struggling Learners.* This three-tape set features Mrs. Hensley in a live workshop setting where she explains the approaches to teaching the special child. A balanced approach is one that contains remediation as well as compensation. Remediation is working on the skills that are at a deficit. Compensation is learning strategies to manage material, such as fewer problems on a page, and such. Finally, I watched the video, *Program Planning for Special Needs Students.* Using her accompanying *Curriculum Planning Resource Guide,* this video took me step-by-step through the process of designing a program and choosing resources to use with my daughter. AVCS operates an umbrella school program, and Mrs. Hensley offers consultation to homeschooling families. AVCS Books has a complete catalog of curriculum materials and resources.

Christian Cottage Schools
Mike and Teri Spray
3560 West Dawson Road
Sedalia, CO 80135
303-688-6626
info@christiancottage.com
www.christiancottage.com
   Teri Spray says:

>       Our purpose is to help parents to feel successful in
> their homeschooling experience. . . . Because we view
> each child as a unique individual, we begin by testing
> each child one-on-one with a nationally standardized
> achievement battery. . . . The parent also completes
> detailed information for us about their family as well as
> the child. Our next step is to meet with the parents
> via phone or face-to-face for a curriculum design. We
> painstakingly develop an education program item by
> item with the parents' input. We will also purchase
> the materials for the family from over 110 different
> suppliers. For enrolling families we include suggestions
> for daily curriculum assignments as well.
>       We like to say that special needs are our specialty!
> Approximately 75 percent of the children we work
> with have some sort of specific learning need. We work
> with almost all special needs including developmental
> delays. Most of the students we help have specific learn-
> ing challenge such as dyslexia, auditory processing prob-
> lems, etc.
>       Everyone tells me my greatest gift is encourage-
> ment. I know that it is a gift from God given to me to
> help others. After the testing, we design prescriptive
> curriculum programs with the parents, and we tailor
> the program to be suited exactly to what the child
> needs. Our goal is for the parent to return to us next

year and say, "We had a great year!" This is our priority, not whether or not the family followed a particular prescription or curriculum program.

We are available throughout the year for counsel and support. We keep a binder handy for each family so anyone can see in a moment exactly which materials the child is using when a parent calls.

My best advice is to tell you, "You can do it!" But you don't have to go it alone. It's okay to get help in the process; you don't have to be lone ranger simply because you chose to remove or keep your child from the school system. However, it is very important for you as the parents to have the final say and authority over all matters pertaining to your child. God has placed parents as the authority over children, not the government. You as a parent understand the needs of your child better than anyone. No one else on this earth loves and understands your child more than you. God gave you this child for a reason and he will not leave you or forsake you in the teaching, training, and parenting of your child.

Joyce Herzog
1500 Albany Street
Schnectady, NY 12304
800-745-8212
www.JoyceHerzog.com

Author of *Scaredy Cat Reading, Learning in Spite of Labels, Choosing and Using Curriculum,* and many more titles. Her Web site has tips and a very active message board. She frequently posts answers to questions on the message board. Also does private consultations and provides help with curriculum planning.

Dr. Joe Sutton
Exceptional Diagnostics
220 Douglas Drive
Simpsonville, SC 29681
www.edtesting.com
864-967-4729
suttonjp@juno.com

Offers tests that parents can administer, such as ADHD screening, LD screening, and career interest tests, as well as in-depth tests and evaluations performed by Dr. Sutton in his home office or in selected major cities. Sutton is the author of *Strategies for Struggling Learners*.

## Endnotes

1. Tom and Sherry Bushnell, *Christian Homes and Special Kids* (Portland, ID: NATHHAN/CHASK, 2003), 4–5 (www.nath han.com).

2. Brian Ray, *Worldwide Guide to Homeschooling* (Nashville, TN: Broadman & Holman, 2003).

3. Steven E. Duvall, D. Lawrence Ward, Joseph C. Delquadri, Charles R. Greenwood, "An Exploratory Study of Home School Instructional Environments and Their Effect on the Basic Skills of Students with Learning Disabilities," *Education and Treatment of Christian*, 20 (1997), 150–72.

4. Roger Pierangelo, PhD and Robert Jacoby, *The Parents' Complete Special Education Guide* (West Nyack, NY: The Center for Applied Research in Education, 1996).

5. "Resource Room," *The Old Schoolhouse Magazine* (Winter 2003), 26.

❋  ❋  ❋

Christine M. Field practiced law for eight years before becoming a full-time mother. She and her husband, Mark, live and homeschool their four children in Wheaton, Illinois, where Mark serves as chief of police. Three of their four children are adopted, one through a private adoption and two from Korea. They are also active foster parents. She is the author of several books, including *Coming Home to Raise Your Children, Should You Adopt?, A Field Guide to Home Schooling, Life Skills for Kids,* and *Help for the Harried Home Schooler.* Her newest book, *Home Schooling the Challenging Child,* was published by B&H Publishing Group in 2005.

She serves as senior correspondent and Resource Room columnist for *The Old Schoolhouse Magazine.* Her work appears regularly at Crosswalk.com, Lifeway.com, *Hearts at Home Magazine,* The Proverbs 31 Homemaker, and others. Her articles on life skills have appeared in *Focus on the Family Magazine* and *Single Parent Family.*

Visit her Web site, The Home Field Advantage, at www. HomeFieldAdvantage.org.

# Homeschooling Our Children with Special Needs

*Sherry Bushnell*

Have you ever tried sweeping up a mess of those little Styrofoam worms in a breeze? In February, gathering together what is left of my imaginative efforts to make homeschooling inspiring is similar.

The Queen of Repetition is my name. This is actually not such a bad thing when it comes to teaching Lynny, my eleven-year-old daughter with autism and cerebral palsy; Jordan, my sixteen-year-old with Down's syndrome; and Sheela, my fifteen-year-old who is blind. I feel a great responsibility to help them reach their full potential. Perhaps it is because they are adopted. Commissioned by God to raise another mother's child is an awesome task.

To make matters more complicated, my expectations for all of them have had to be readjusted many times. My assumption that they would succeed in different areas has actually stood in the way of the development of their true abilities. Let me explain: Sheela, born without eyes, was adopted into our home and hearts with the full trust that she was otherwise normal mentally. As she grew older, the gap widened between her abilities and others her age. I thought the reason for this was me—my teaching techniques, my choice of homeschool materials, my parenting skills. All of these "failures" weighed me down for many years like an eighty-pound sack of wheat berries on my shoulder.

My dreams and goals were too high. God made Sheela mildly mentally disabled. Instead of rejoicing in her ability to read at a second-grade level, I mourned over her inability to comprehend numbers. Instead of marveling over her patience, perseverance, and eagerness to please, I sweated over the fact she only liked to play with the five-year-olds. God gently helped me face her limitations by showing me mine. It was my pride.

Giving the Lord room to fashion Sheela into a woman of God meant giving over my selfish expectations for Sheela. I will never forget my tears over her seeming stubbornness in not doing a math assignment involving simple numbers, one to ten. It didn't make any sense. She seemed so mature in other areas. Yet this task she failed again and again. I was angry. My husband wisely suggested we just drop the task, moving on to something else. After my attitude improved, we might try again. We never officially tried again. There are ways to get around without having to comprehend numbers over five. Instead of adding, we might make sure everyone has a place setting at the table, or that all the boys have a given number of socks in their basket, or that everyone has a bowl of soup and a piece of bread.

Now take Jordan for instance. Having Down's syndrome makes him a special treasure. He is healthy, strong, and a real help in the house. Yet he cannot print his name, the ABCs, or even my name, M-o-m. Now how can our family be an outstanding testimony of the benefits of homeschooling a child with

Down's syndrome? So many people are watching for the results of teaching our children with special needs. Jordan is diagnosed as severely mentally impaired. How do we teach him? Neither my husband nor I have a college degree. There is no such thing as a curriculum for children with Down's syndrome.

Our love for our son and our strong desire to see him succeed is enough. Giving God the credit for how wonderful Jordan is turning out keeps me from getting too proud. I am pleased with Jordan's happy heart, uninfected with the world's idea of self-love and gratification. He is caring, helpful, and knows he is loved by his family. I think Jordan is the Lord's way of reminding me that his creation is always a blessing. Our perception of life and our goals for our children need to equal his.

Little Lynny is truly a miracle. How God can reach down into a child's heart and mind, healing for his purposes, amazes me. Born to a fourteen-year-old girl in India (Lynny's mother and father are brother and sister), she was injured and left to die in a soggy ditch. The Lord plucked baby Lynny out of the muck and set her in our home. We wanted a sister for Sheela who was also blind. We thought it would be nice for them to grow up together. Her medical record stated that she was blind and hearing impaired. She is neither. Autism and moderate/severe cerebral palsy put Lynny in a unique category.

In the end it all worked out really well, for Lynny acts as Sheela's eyes, and Sheela is Lynny's legs and hands. They are a good team for helping around the house. But early on we struggled. As an active family, we purposely chose not to pick a child with mobility limitations. We loved to bike, go to the beach, and be otherwise unhampered by pushing a wheelchair. For years I grumbled in my heart. Should we have let her go to another family? Looking back, I can now see God's perfect plan for my life. Just as Lynny needs us to care for her basic functions, we need Lynny's limitations to perfect us. Now I cherish our growth of character development. We are learning better how to put others first, denying our selfish desires and letting God plan our lives. Life would have been easier if we had chosen to let her go, but by God's grace we are obeying him. Surprise . . . we still bike, go to the ocean, and camp!

Homeschooling Lynny, with her different needs, has not been what most would consider "schooling." Our first big question was, how can we help this little girl, whose mind and body are damaged? She lay crying in frustration and fear all day. How could we reach her? We knew that Jesus died for Lynny and loves her dearly. We came to the conclusion that we can love her too; laying down our lives for his child whom he made—whatever that would take.

Ministering to the heart of a child who is disabled means more than warm hugs and good food. It means more than potty training, ABCs, or even teaching reading and math. With all that it does involve, we know that in our home, without the Lord to guide us, we could never succeed.

Lynny's attitude and perception of life hampered her first six years of growth. It even prevented her from happily eating, being potty trained, learning her letters, and communicating. Through Lynny God taught me that character development is the most important issue in a child's life. Our special-needs children will always live with someone. I want my children to be a blessing to their caregiver.

In all of our children, we want to see a desire to please—even in the eyes of our special needs children. Until then teaching academics is fruitless. Obedience to simple requests is more important than learning to point out the letters of the alphabet. Both can happen at once, but we know that overlooking a crummy attitude will not produce the fruit of righteousness.

How excited we are when our children catch on to new concepts. We feel good about homeschooling and our choice of materials. But the balance will eventually come when we are dealing with mental and physical delays. For instance, a mom, who is struggling to find out how to repeat the first grade for her child for the fourth time, knows by now that there is no cure-all curriculum that will eliminate her child's disabilities. It is the acceptance of where our children are functioning that makes homeschooling a joy.

God's ways are wiser than ours. He takes pleasure in fine-tuning sweetness in a sixteen-year-old girl who struggles with fractions. He delights in polishing the ten-year-old son who diligently obeys his parents yet cannot read.

Our job as homeschooling parents is to observe just exactly how his beautiful creation, his child on loan to us, can be taught to be an example of Christ's love. When our children are eighteen, what will matter most? Honestly, their ability to read and do math at the third-grade level will not be as important as their willingness to work hard and be on time. Disability in the world's eyes runs on two levels: (1) able to function, (2) not able to function. Reading may not count as much when it comes to holding down a job for the disabled. Working hard and having a good attitude make them functional.

Can I share with you my secret for getting my family through homeschooling with success? Prayer brings results. To this day God has answered each of our concerns about homeschooling, whether it be our lack of finances for therapy equipment, how to help a child reach the next step, or even open our blind eyes to our crummy attitudes. Our requests are often answered within days of our heartfelt plea.

On the subject of work, how about sweeping up those Styrofoam worms in a breeze? A quick solution is a spray of water. It secures those flighty pieces until they can be swept into the dustpan with a good broom. Just like a hard-to-clean-up mess secured, God's peace and his Word anchor my scattered thoughts, my burnout, my lack of resolve and resourcefulness into successes.

We encourage those who are homeschooling children with disabilities to bravely ask God to bring about clarity, education solutions, equipment, and even patience! His solutions are much better than we ever dreamed.

May the Lord help all of us to be able to adjust to God's vision for our children. May we be able to adjust to the blossoming of their true abilities.

Tom and Sherry Bushnell homeschool their eleven children in beautiful northern Idaho. From their home they operate NATHHAN, the National Challenged Homeschoolers, and CHASK, Christian Homes and Special Kids. NATHHAN supports families homeschooling children with disabilities of all kinds. CHASK is a ministry that finds unborn babies with special needs and gives birth parents encouragement either to raise their child or place the child for adoption instead of aborting. Contact the Bushnells at NATHHAN/CHASK, PO Box 39, Porthill, ID 83853, 208-267-6246, www.nathhan.com.

# Carschooling®

*The Lord GOD hath given me the tongue of the
learned, that I should know how to speak a word in
season to him that is weary: he wakeneth morning by
morning, he wakeneth mine ear to hear as the
learned. The Lord GOD hath opened mine ear, and
I was not rebellious, neither turned away back.*

—ISAIAH 50:4–5

✻ ✻ ✻

*In traveling, a man must carry knowledge with
him if he would bring home knowledge.*

—SAMUEL JOHNSON

As every parent knows, having active children means playing
chauffeur. Homeschool families have to factor in time
spent on the road while running errands, transporting family
members to church, social functions, support group meetings,
doctor and dentist appointments—the list goes on! While being

together as a family for most of the day means a better student-to-teacher ratio for homeschool families, it also means that most of the family will be present, if not directly involved, with the tasks that need to be accomplished each day. For those who have older children involved in multiple activities, the day or week can be a round-robin of road trips. Whether it's a trip to the grocery store, a planned educational field trip, or the annual family vacation, more and more homeschool families find themselves in the car. For better or worse, these trips must be taken, and rather than allowing her time in the car to be wasted hours, Diane Flynn Keith has chosen to make the time educational and fun.

Most homeschool parents will agree that a major point of home education is recognizing that learning takes place everywhere. While some families choose to have their children sit at school desks to work on their lessons, others gather around the kitchen table, while still others sprawl on blankets in the backyard to learn. Those who grew up taking an annual trip across the country in the back of a station wagon can attest that learning occurs there as well! Making efficient use of the many hours spent in our vehicles with our children is one way we can define the Carschooling® approach.

Carschooling® is not just about making sure the math books are in the trunk and the calculator is floating around under someone's seat. This approach is all about having an adventurous mind-set and a willingness to be prepared for educational opportunities. By taking the time to coin the phrase *Carschooling*®, Diane Flynn Keith has offered homeschoolers a term to describe what many do in their day or week. Whether most of your time is spent on the road from one activity to the next or Carschooling® simply supplements your primary educational method, the end result is the same: having planned activities and accessible supplies will encourage further educational forays that allow your family to make the most of their time in their seat belts.

# Carschooling® Takes Homeschooling on the Road!

## Diane Flynn Keith

On-the-go homeschoolers can convert their cars into mobile classrooms to make the most of every homeschool mile. I call this conversion Carschooling®. Whether you are running a five-minute errand or taking a five-hundred-mile road trip, Carschooling® helps you easily and effectively use time spent in the car to turn your kids into "roads scholars."

You can find teaching moments by just being aware of what is in your environment, particularly when you are traveling in the car. Language arts, math, science, history, geography, art, music, and even physical education are among the curriculum components you can explore in your automobile.

For example, my sons got antsy after riding in the backseat of our car for more than twenty minutes. They started to fuss or argue, and I found myself trying to drive and referee simultaneously. Diverting their attention to find interesting things along the road changed the atmosphere in the car and resulted in some really cooperative learning adventures. I'd point out cows on a hillside and challenge them to identify and count animals spied along the road for the next five minutes or five miles. I'd ask them to look for geometrical figures in road signs. I'd tell them to find parts of speech on billboards by searching for nouns, verbs, adjectives, and so on. Occasionally, I'd notice a historical marker and pull over to let the kids stand on the exact spot where a famous Spanish explorer camped with his expedition long ago. These activities not only solved the "he's touching me" gripe temporarily; they also led to memorable conversations that boosted the children's knowledge of the world.

## Games and Activities for Every Subject

Carschooling® goes way beyond the familiar car bingo when it comes to activities that augment learning and cover national curriculum standards. From memorizing multiplication tables to exploring flattened fauna, here is an array of fun ways to learn on the go.

## Language Arts

Here are a few ideas designed to improve reading, writing, spelling, and grammar skills while traveling in the car.

### BILLBOARD ABCs

Pick a letter of the alphabet (for example, *D*) and ask young carschoolers to look for that letter or words that start with the letter on billboards. Or make the sound of a letter of the alphabet (for example "buh" for *B*) and ask them to find pictures of things with names that begin with that sound.

### Drive-by Dictionary Definitions

*Note*: You will need a pencil and paper to keep track of scores and a pocket dictionary.

Search for a new vocabulary word on billboards that your carschoolers don't know. Say the word out loud and let them guess the meaning. Then use the word in a sentence. Have each carschooler suggest a definition of the word. Ask everyone to vote for the definition they think is correct. Look up the definition of the word in the dictionary and read it out loud. Each carschooler earns one point for selecting the correct definition. The person with the most points at the end of the game wins.

### *Extra Credit*

- Ask your carschoolers to suggest synonyms and antonyms.
- Spell the words used in the game and have your carschoolers write them down in a notebook along with the definitions.

### Taking Turns with Stories

Storytelling develops listening skills and improves reading and writing proficiency. Start telling a story. Each time you make a sharp right or left turn, pass the story to another passenger and ask them to tell what happens next. Use a tape recorder to record the tale as it's being told, and you'll have a fun family story to listen to again and again!

## Math

Carschooling® is the perfect time to demonstrate to your kids that math is everywhere from the dashboard to the toll-booth. Here are some fun math activities and resources to help you survive the drive without the textbook drill and kill.

COUNTING GAMES

The miles seem to whiz by with these counting and number identification games:

- Choose a general category such as things that are yellow or round, or a more specific topic like trucks or cows, and see how many your carschoolers can count while looking out the window.
- Pick one number, and challenge your carschoolers to count how many times they can find it on mileage signs, license plates, billboards, and at gas stations.

MULTIPLICATION IS A BIG DEAL

Take a regular deck of playing cards and remove the face cards and jokers. Shuffle the cards and deal them all out, face down, between two carschoolers. Have each player turn over the top card from their deck at the same time. Multiply (in their heads) the numbers represented on the two cards and call out the answer. For example, player one turns over the 8 of spades and player two flips over the 3 of diamonds. Multiply 8 x 3 to get the answer 24. The first person to call out the correct answer gets to keep the two turned-over cards. Play continues until all the cards have been used. Whoever has the most cards at the end of the game wins!

ROAMIN' NUMERALS

Challenge your carschoolers to convert speed limit signs into Roman numerals. For example, if you spot a 25 MPH speed limit sign, call out the number 25 in Roman numerals or XXV. If you see a 50 MPH sign, call out L. Here are some of the more common Roman numerals and their numeric equivalents:

1 = I, 2 = II, 3 = III, 4 = IV, 5 = V, 10 = X, 50 = L, 100 = C, 500 = D, 1000 = M

*Extra Credit*

You can also convert license plate numerals. Give each player a paper and pencil. Pick out a license plate on a passing car and write down the numerals (ignore the letters). Let's say the license plate was WR534G. Remove the letters and write down 534. Convert 534 into Roman Numerals or DXXXIV.

## PIPE CLEANER GEOMETRY

Pipe cleaners are the perfect geometric math manipulative. Bendable, colorful, and connectable, pipe cleaners can become any shape you can think of to make. Just pass the pipe cleaners around and ask, "Who can make a triangle?" Have the kids make a square, rectangle, circle, diamond, trapezoid, parallelogram, pentagon, octagon, and a star shape too! Once they've made a geometric shape, try to match it to something they see out the car window (for example, a yield sign is a triangle shape, a stop sign is an octagon, etc.). For a real challenge ask the kids to figure out how to make three-dimensional shapes, like cubes, spheres, and cones. Pipe cleaners can also be shaped into numbers and letters.

Pipe cleaners are available in many sizes and colors. Inexpensive pipe cleaners in bulk containers can be found at arts and crafts stores. Klutz Press (www.klutz.com) offers activity kits with pipe cleaners that are perfect for road trips:

- *Pipe Cleaners Gone Crazy: A Complete Guide to Bending Fuzzy Sticks* by Laura Torres
- *Big Fat Pipe Cleaners* by the Klutz Press Staff

## Science

Your car is a portable science laboratory, and Mother Nature provides all of the materials and specimens you will need to learn biology, zoology, botany, entomology, and more. Stock your mobile laboratory with a few scientific tools and get ready to turn your road trips into science expeditions.

## MAGNIFY IT!

Having a magnifying glass for each carschooler is not an extravagance but an essential learning tool that will help to eliminate the whine in drive time. Encourage your children to find scientific mementos of your trip each time you stop along the way. Keep sealable plastic bags in the car and use them to collect rocks, feathers, leaves, flowers, nuts, seeds, pods, dead bugs, moss, and other natural treasures. Have your carschoolers examine their finds with a magnifying glass and discuss the details of what they see. Ask them to sketch their specimens and note any observations next to the drawing. This provides an experiential lesson in the scientific method of observation and recording. Use field guides to extend the learning.

## FINDING FLATTENED FAUNA

The Latin word for animals is *fauna*. Another name for *road kill* is *flattened fauna*, and we've come up with an activity that's sure to spark the kids' interest and pass the time while covering subjects like zoology and Latin. You will need an animal field guide as well as an English-Latin pocket dictionary. You will also need a small notebook and pencil for each carschooler.

Have the kids look for flattened fauna on the road. When they see it, tell them to point it out and identify it, and then write the name of the animal down in the notebook. Then, look up the animal in the field guide and find the Latin name for it. Tell them to write the Latin name (or scientific name) next to the English name.

Look up the Latin name in the English-Latin dictionary and discover how to pronounce it correctly. Take turns pronouncing the Latin name of the animal.

If there are long stretches of road between flattened fauna sightings, have the kids draw a picture of the animal under the name in their notebook while someone reads the information in the field guide about the animal.

Each time the carschoolers see flattened fauna, have them follow the same procedure. Keep your notebooks, field guide, and dictionary in the car and add to your list on subsequent trips. Add living fauna sightings to the notebook as well. By the way, if you are on the road and have a laptop with Internet access, you can find a free online field guide at http://www.enature.com/guides/select_group.asp

## History

Your tax dollars supply exceptional roadside history text-books called "historical markers." Don't pass them by. Stop, read, and learn. You will find that reading a commemorative plaque about one historical incident will ignite your carschoolers' interest in other history topics. Here are some more innovative ways to study history on the road.

### ROAD TRIP PICTURE TIME LINE

For this activity you will need a Polaroid camera; a notebook; glue or Scotch tape; and a pen. Tell your carschoolers that they are going to make a pictorial history time line of your road trip. Because the starting point of your trip is home, have the kids take a picture of your family at home. Put the picture on the first page of your photo album or notebook to represent the start of your trip, and write the date next to the photo. Each time you stop along the way, take a picture of where you stop or, alternately, purchase picture postcards of the places you visit at souvenir shops. Glue or tape the picture to the notebook, and write the date and the name of the place you visited next to the picture. Be sure to put each picture in chronological order, creating a historical record or time line of your trip. Invite the kids to write notes next to the pictures to remind themselves of something memorable that happened there.

Your children will begin to understand that history is really just the record of things that happen in succession in people's lives. Current history is the record of what is happening day by day in your children's lives. As your trip progresses, review the photo time line and point out that the pictures you took three days ago are your children's *past history.* When the trip is over and you arrive home, remove the pages of the notebook (keeping them in chronological order) and hang them in order on a wall. Then walk along your history time line and recollect the highlights of your trip. Your kids will have a much greater understanding of what history is all about.

CHANGING HISTORY

Have everyone in the car search their purses, pockets, and seat cushions for spare change. Put all of the change in one container. Pass the container and have each carschooler withdraw one coin. Each player takes a turn telling the others one historical fact about a person, place, or thing depicted on the coin, or they may relate a historical event that took place the year that is imprinted on the coin. For example if a carschooler draws a penny, he may say that the penny has a picture of Abraham Lincoln who was assassinated at the Ford Theater. If the year imprinted on the coin is 1963, she may say that was the year President Kennedy was assassinated. To give you a head start, here are some facts about the most common U.S. coins.

## Lincoln Penny

- The front features a profile of Abraham Lincoln, sixteenth President of the United States and signer of the Emancipation Proclamation that ended slavery.
- The back features the Lincoln Memorial, a monument in Washington, D.C. (Use a magnifying glass to see Lincoln sitting inside the Lincoln Memorial.)

## Jefferson Nickel with Monticello

- The front features a profile of Thomas Jefferson, the third President of the United States and primary author of the Declaration of Independence.
- The back features Monticello, the estate where Jefferson lived in Virginia.

## Jefferson Nickel with Lewis and Clark Commemorative (2003–2005)

- The front features a profile of Thomas Jefferson.
- The back depicts historic images of Lewis and Clark's expedition.

## Roosevelt Dime with Torch

- The front features a profile of Franklin Delano Roosevelt, the only U.S. President to serve four terms of office.
- The back features a picture of a torch with an olive branch on the left and an oak branch on the right.

## Washington Quarter with Eagle

- The front features a profile of George Washington, the first U.S. President.
- The back features a picture of the presidential coat of arms—an eagle with spread wings.

## 50 State Quarters with Washington (1999–2008)

- The front features a profile of George Washington.
- The back depicts one of the fifty states.

### AUDIO BIOGRAPHIES

Print out the free Carschool® Calendar at www.Carschooling. com to find important historical events for each day of the year. On a day you will be driving a lot, refer to the calendar and choose an event for that day (like the birthday of a famous scientist, musician, or author). Go to the library and find an audio biography of that person. Play the CD or tape while you are driving in the car that day.

Note: Audio Bookshelf (www.audiobookshelf.com) produces an entire audio biographical book series by Kathleen Krull that the whole family will enjoy. The Web site includes free, printable "Curricular Connections" for the series that includes:

- **Lives of the Presidents: Fame, Shame (and What the Neighbors Thought)**—Listen to the tell-all accounts about the interesting and surprising behavior of Presidents and First Ladies.
- **Lives of Extraordinary Women: Rulers, Rebels**—Twenty biographies of women in history from Cleopatra to Eleanor Roosevelt.
- **Lives of the Writers: Comedies, Tragedies**—Featuring the lives and literature of nineteen writers from Cervantes to Langston Hughes.
- **Lives of the Musicians: Good Times, Bad Times**—Twenty composers from Beethoven to Guthrie are profiled with samples of their music.
- **Lives of the Artists: Masterpieces and Messes**—From Da Vinci to Warhol, listen to the biographies of twenty artists and their artistic accomplishments.

## Geography

No subject lends itself more to car travel than geography, from reading maps to studying landscapes. Point out formations and introduce geographic terminology including mountains, lakes, rivers, peninsulas, islands, capes, and more. You can find lots of books, interactive games, and study guides on geography through the National Geography Bee Web site at: www.national geographic.com/geographybee. Here's a geography game and a resource to try in the car with your family.

### FRUIT-FLAVORED GEOGRAPHY

Planning to pack lunches for the road? Slip an unusual fruit into your children's lunch bags. When they discover it, discuss the country of its origin. Keep an atlas or an inflatable globe* in the car. Have your children locate the country. Talk about the climate, the people, the language, and the culture. If you don't know much about that country, look it up on the Internet or at the library before your trip. Get an audiotape of that country's traditional music at your library and listen while you have lunch in the car. Here are some interesting fruit selections to get you started:

- **Guava—Peru.** Archaeologists discovered guava seeds in dig sites that were several thousand years old.
- **Kiwi—China.** Also known as Chinese gooseberries. Introduced to New Zealand in 1934, which is now the undisputed kiwifruit capital of the world. The brown, fuzzy kiwifruit received its name because it resembles New Zealand's national bird, the kiwi.
- **Mango—India.** Mangoes were transported to Africa during the sixteenth century and carried aboard Portuguese ships to Brazil in the 1700s. By 1742, mangoes were found growing in the West Indies.

- **Papaya—Panama and Colombia.** It was found there by Spanish explorers and first mentioned in their chronicles in 1526.
- **Passion fruit—Brazil.** Brazil is the country of origin, and the fruit was eventually introduced to other tropical regions by European explorers.
- **Pomegranate—Middle East and Asia.** Now commonly grown in Africa, India, Malaysia, southern Europe, and California and Arizona in the United States.
- **Star fruit (also called carambola)—Southeast Asia** is the place of origin.

\* *Inflatable globes* are fantastic to use in the car because they are soft (and therefore safe), and deflate for easy storage in the glove compartment. You can find them at Einstein's Emporium 800-522-8281 or www.einsteins-emporium.com.

## Art and Music

Stock your carschool with tools that will encourage the students to produce works of art. Include plenty of paper, markers, safety scissors, glue, clay, modeling wax, coloring books, window paints, and anything else that inspires artistic expression.

You can also stock your car with music courtesy of your local library audiovisual department and the Internet. Explore different musical genres and composers for a well-rounded music education. Look for the Classical Kids audio recordings that include titles such as *Beethoven Lives Upstairs*, *Mr. Bach Comes to Call*, *Mozart's Magic Fantasy*, and *Vivaldi's Ring of Mystery*. Try the following ideas too.

### Post-It Note Art Gallery

Post-It Notes are great to use for car activities because they will stick to seat backs and windows. Get a variety of sizes and colors. Use them to tally scores or for games like tic-tac-toe and hangman. Kids can also draw pictures on the notes and decorate the car with their own Post-It Note art exhibit.

## MUSICAL ART!

This activity is great for toddlers to teens! Give everyone in the car a sturdy art notepad with blank paper and some crayons. Turn on some music and tell them to draw or scribble along with the music. Whatever pictures, images, strokes of the crayon (squiggles, dots, lines, etc.), or colors the music sparks in their imagination is what they should put on their paper. Pop music drumbeats may result in rhythmic lines. Children's tunes like "Somewhere over the Rainbow" may lead to pictures of what the song is about. Just let the music guide them to create images that depict it. Write the name of the song that inspired their work on the back of the drawing. Keep the notepads in the car, and try different kinds of music on each car trip. Listen to classical, rock, jazz, children's tunes, and others, and compare the pictures the music inspires in each carschooling artist.

***Note: Sing-Along Resource!***

A family sing-along is just the thing to encourage a love of music and make those miles whiz by. *All American CAR-I-OKE* by David Schiller is the popular game of karaoke for the car! You get a CD of fun, instrumental songs and three lyric books to guide you in singing along to such popular tunes as "Proud Mary," "Give My Regards to Broadway," and "Danny Boy."

## Physical Education

Getting some physical exercise in the car is not as difficult as it might seem, and giving the kids a chance to shake out their sillies can be crucial to maintaining the driver's sanity. Here's an innovative idea for exercising with seat belts securely fastened.

## CAR SEAT EXERCISES

There are videos and DVDs by fitness gurus offering exercises for people whose movement is constricted or who are confined to wheelchairs. All of the exercises are done sitting down. If you have a video or DVD player in your car or a laptop computer, you can do aerobic exercise in the car. The routines feature a variety of arm movements and optional leg swings. Richard Simmons offers a popular title, *Sit Tight*, with easy-to-follow instructions and upbeat music that kids will enjoy.

## More Carschooling®

I hope this tip-of-the-iceberg view of Carschooling® activities and resources demonstrates how families can make the most of every homeschool mile. For more information and resources, get the book *Carschooling: Over 350 Entertaining Games and Activities to Turn Travel Time into Learning Time* by Diane Flynn Keith, published by Three Rivers Press, a division of Random House. Visit the Carschooling® Web site at www. Carschooling.com to get free games, resource suggestions, and a free Carschooling® calendar! Come to a Carschooling® Workshop or arrange to have a presentation at your next homeschool conference. Share your ideas and resources for Carschooling® by emailing Editor@Homefires.com.

Diane Flynn Keith has homeschooled her two sons for four-teen years in the San Francisco Bay area. She is the editor of Homefires.com, an online journal and resource center for home-school families. Diane is a popular writer and speaker on the topic of homeschooling. She is a featured columnist for *The Link National Homeschool Newspaper* and has written for *Home Education Magazine, The Old Schoolhouse Magazine, Practical Homeschooling, The California Homeschooler,* and many more publications. She has contributed to a number of books on home-schooling including *The Homeschooling Almanac, The California Homeschool Guide,* and *The Ultimate Book of Homeschooling Ideas.* She is the author of *Carschooling: Over 350 Entertaining Games and Activities to Turn Travel Time into Learning Time,* published by Random House. Diane is also the publisher of ClickSchooling, a free daily e-service that provides recommen-dations for great educational Web sites on the Net.

Most recently, Diane has organized opposition to govern-ment mandatory preschool through her Web site, www.Universal Preschool.com. You can contact her at: Editor@Homefires.com or visit: www.Homefires.com and www.Carschooling.com.

# Eclectic Method

*Study to show thyself approved unto God,
a workman that needeth not to be ashamed,
rightly dividing the word of truth.*

—2 TIMOTHY 2:15

*My advice is always to let the interests and the
inclinations of the children determine what happens
and to give children access to as much of the parents'
lives and the world around them as possible, given
your own circumstances, so that children have the
widest possible range of things to look at and think
about. See which things interest them most, and help
them to go down that particular road.*

—JOHN HOLT

As different as the educational methods used by homeschoolers are, the resources available are exponentially more

diverse. Even when a family finally finds a homeschooling method that they believe will suit their needs, a wealth of products and curricula wait. Walking through the vendor hall of a homeschool convention makes one wonder, *What should I use and how should I use it? It all looks so wonderful!* Knowing that every product is not going to suit our needs is important. More important, though, is to know that it is perfectly acceptable to mix and match products and resources that best suit the needs of our children in our efforts to educate them. Gleaning wisdom from one book about homeschooling, adapting an approach that better suits our child's strengths or challenges, and collecting products from a variety of sources allow many homeschoolers to create their own eclectic mix of educational methods and supplies.

This eclectic approach even varies from one family to the next. One homeschool parent may crave the structure of the classical method but realize that her heart tells her a more child-focused method will work better for her young children. The focus on service and delayed academics of the Moore Formula may suit a relaxed homeschool family, but a student's sudden interest in languages will require the use of a classical Latin curriculum. Some eclectic families focus more on the resources themselves, choosing to supplement traditional textbooks with unit studies, creating a springboard from a single chapter in a history book to a full-blown unit complete with a grand finale field trip to a historical site. Being able to hold to what works and shed what doesn't is empowering for both the teacher and the students in the homeschool. The ability to integrate the various approaches and philosophies frees the eclectic homeschool family to enjoy their educational journey. As overwhelming as it can be to sift through the many choices in educational products available, eclectic homeschoolers can feel confident in combining resources as opposed to feeling they are betraying their method's requirements by slipping in a nature walk here or a textbook there.

Maggie Hogan of Bright Ideas Press joins us to share the smorgasbord that is eclectic homeschooling, while Diana Waring of History Alive! introduces us to various types of learners and how to adapt to their learning styles. In the spirit of the eclectic approach, be prepared to take away that which works for you.

# Eclectic Homeschooling

## Maggie S. Hogan with Tyler Hogan

Picture this: you're standing in a buffet line with so much food you don't know where to start. With plate in hand, you stare at the multitude of meats, pastas, salads, seafood, Chinese dishes, vegetables, and pastries. A waiter comes up and asks, "Have you decided which one dish you will have tonight?" "What?" you say. "What do you mean one? This is a smorgasbord, isn't it?" "Yes, of course," he replies, "you can eat whatever and however much you want, but you can only have one dish. Enjoy your meal!"

Ridiculous, isn't it? How can they expect you to choose just one thing to eat? Isn't that missing the point of a buffet: getting a little bit of everything?

Just like a grand buffet, there is a huge variety of great programs, courses, books, and curricula in the homeschool market, each of which appeals to different learning and teaching styles, family schedules, level of teacher involvement, and more. Smorgasbord homeschooling allows us to pick and choose what works best for our family.

We've been picking delicacies from the homeschool smorgasbord for years. We've kept notebooks, taken classical languages, had online tutors, done research projects and apprenticeships, been in co-ops, participated in church programs, and even occasionally used textbooks. They are all valid components of a fine education, and our children have benefited tremendously from having a wide variety of experiences.

Because *smorgasbord homeschooling* sounds like a Swedish cooking school, I prefer to call our method the eclectic approach. (Note to self: enough with the food analogies—I'm getting hungry.)

## Warning 1

In giving you a window into our homeschool world, I encourage you not to mimic exactly what we do. Use it as a springboard as you pray about, brainstorm, and consider how you want your homeschool to look. God made all of our families unique, and homeschools will naturally reflect that uniqueness.

## Warning 2

Repeat after me: We will not try to do everything in one year! When I give workshops and show samples of various homeschooling projects we've enjoyed, I have to remind everyone that I'm looking back over many years of homeschooling. Attempting to weave all these ideas together into one year will not make you a basket; it will make you a basket case!

Bob and I have two sons who have now both graduated. They're well-adjusted young adults, living productive lives. JB is in the army, and Tyler is in college. Having reached this milestone of homeschooling, I can let you in on a little secret: choosing the right spelling program is not going to have any long-term significance.

Don't waste time fretting over which curriculum to choose. Pray about it, discuss it with your spouse, then make a decision, and move on. If it turns out not to work, you can always change later.

## Favorite Homeschool Memories

What will your kids look back on and say they loved about homeschooling? Ask them! Here are some of our favorite memories:

- Making a 3-D Jell-O cell
- Writer's co-op 10 years
- Reading
- Having friends over
- Serving at church
- Traveling
- Mission trips
- Internships
- Earning money
- Making books
- Playing games
- Talking/discussing
- Music
- J. R. R. Tolkein
- Mini-marshmallows and chocolate chips
- Being creative
- Making displays
- Building forts

What do they love to do? Do it more! What do they dislike? Is there a way to make it more palatable? For example, we wouldn't, of course, drop math, but we finally let our youngest choose his own math curriculum—much to his satisfaction.

People wonder if I "make up" my own curriculum. Although I have written or pulled together much of what we've used, we have also enjoyed ready-made materials. A wealth of wonderful homeschool options is available now. Here are some of the ways we've homeschooled:

- Co-ops
- Local tutoring
- Internet tutoring
- Video courses
- Computer courses
- Textbooks
- Internships
- College classes
- CLEP tests
- Self-study
- Exchange program
- One-on-one with mom or dad

Bob and I see ourselves as facilitators of our sons' education. This means we don't always have to be the experts. I don't know Latin or Spanish, and yet our boys received Latin and Spanish classes courtesy of women who did know these languages. I never formally taught them logic, either. Tyler read a book that included a video presentation, enjoyed it, and learned the rudiments of logic. JB took his logic course online with a live video-conferencing system, which allowed him both to see and hear the teacher and interact with the other students. He was even able to participate in a live debate!

## A Typical Day

Each eclectic homeschool will look different. Mine doesn't look like Terri Camp's for many reasons, not just because I don't have eight kids! I have spent several weekends in hotel rooms with Terri while we were speaking together. It was great fun hearing her and a few of her children talk about a typical day in their life. So now I will be transparent as well.

## A Peek into Our Homeschool

Travel back in time to our first year of homeschooling. JB was nine, and Tyler was four. Being totally new and ignorant, I didn't even know there was such a thing as homeschooling curriculum. Here's what we did that first year:

Math—JB used a math textbook recommended by a friend of ours who loved math. (Wow! Can you imagine?) She agreed to tutor him once a week if I would do science experiments with her kids. Deal!

English—We read lots and lots of books aloud, and JB read many more to himself. We joined a writers workshop, which we loved and kept up for years. JB wrote stories; I helped him to edit them. He built dioramas and made posters telling about books he read. We learned about favorite authors and practiced grammar as it came up in our writing and reading. I forgot to do spelling. (Note to self: Bob is not a fan of "invented" spelling.) Vocabulary was easy with all the reading we did. JB really took to word processing this year as he hated handwriting.

Science—JB chose four different science topics for us to explore. Chemistry was a favorite! We did lots of experiments, but I didn't do nearly enough explaining about the whys of what happened. (Note to self: next time, explode the volcano outside.) We also used his Boy Scout badges that pertained to science as part of our school day.

History—We found out that JB had received virtually no history in his last three years of public school. I asked him what he would like to learn. He chose Middle Ages and Ancient

Rome. (Think knights and gladiators. Go figure.) I had enough sense at least to teach them in chronological order. Knowing little about either topic, I had great fun reading with him. We did lots of library research, built models, and made a costume. (I don't sew, but I can use duct tape!)

Geography—We put up maps and talked about where things happened, both in history and in current events. We learned map-reading skills, got lost, worked more on map-reading skills. Wished there were great homeschool geography materials available. (Note to self: write a geography book.)

Spanish—Through a rather bizarre set of circumstances, JB spent two mornings a week at the public elementary school acting as an interpreter for a young Mexican boy who spoke no English. This sharpened JB's skills and helped remind him why he liked homeschooling so much: no work sheets or bullies.

Physical education—Homeschool roller skating days, swim lessons at the YMCA, and soccer league.

Bible—The boys and I went to community Bible study (CBS) once a week where the boys participated in a homeschool class. This was in addition to Bible at home and church activities.

Schedule—Try to be up and dressed by 7:00 because if I want our car that day I have to drive Bob to work. If not, I can sleep in until Tyler drags me out of bed. Get JB up by 8:00 a.m. OK, maybe by 9:00. Get breakfast stuff out. (Note to self: do not stay up half the night reading again!)

The little boy I babysit for will show up by 8:00. He and Tyler are friends and will spend the morning playing fairly well together, allowing me to help JB as needed and take care of morning household chores. The boys are responsible for their bedrooms, bathroom, and laundry. I give them time to do this during school. If it is a co-op day or CBS, we have to get up earlier to get ready. JB and I are not morning people, so this is a challenge. (JB says he *is* a morning person—if he only lived in Hong Kong.)

Afternoon—Lunch, quiet time in rooms. The boys usually build with legos. JB also reads during this time. I rest my ears from my verbally gifted children.

Later afternoon—I work on either reading or math skills with Tyler. He is not interested in phonics but loves for me to read to him. He usually needs to have something in his hands to fiddle with while I am reading. He dictates stories to me for writers workshop. Once a week we usually do a little science experiment together. JB finishes up whatever he didn't get done in the morning and also spends time on Scouts stuff.

Tyler tends to get out of sorts late in the afternoon. When I am on top of things, I fix a healthy snack for him. Sometimes he gets to watch a video.

Evenings—Family time. We have an exchange student from Paraguay living with us this year, and he will come home from school and tell us about his day. JB might have soccer practice or Scouts as well. Dinner with dad is a time of discussion and planning. Often a lesson in manners is needed here as well. After dinner Bob reads to the boys from a devotional book, and we spend time discussing it and praying.

Bath time, read aloud time, bedtime! (Note to self: remember to spend time with Bob!)

## Fast-Forward to Today

Each year our homeschooling looked a little different. Depending on the boys' needs, opportunities available, and Bob's input, our homeschool would change to fit the circumstances. Flexibility and dependence on the Lord for wisdom are both key.

But now let's drop the question of what you are using to teach your children and look at homeschooling from a bigger perspective. I have learned that homeschooling should be a lot more about character than curriculum.

I'd like to ask you these four questions:

1. What are your priorities, and do you live your life in a way that accurately reflects them?
2. Are you in the Word daily?
3. Is your prayer life alive?
4. Do you have your eyes fixed on Jesus?

Why am I asking you this in a homeschooling chapter on eclectic homeschooling? Because if this part of your life isn't working, your homeschooling won't work either. I saved the most important part for last because I want you to walk away remembering this:

- Homeschooling is not about the perfect plan.
- Homeschooling is not about the perfect curriculum.
- Homeschooling is not about the perfect family.
- Homeschooling is about having our hearts right with Jesus and passing that love of the Lord on to our kids.
- Homeschooling is a tool for training disciples of Christ, and if, like our smorgasbord at the beginning of our story, you could choose only one dish, that would be the dish to choose.
- God bless you on your journey!

Maggie and Bob Hogan live in Dover, Delaware, where they began homeschooling their two (now grown) sons in 1991. She's a nationally known speaker, a regular columnist for several homeschooling publications, and coauthor of *The Ultimate Geography and Timeline Guide, Gifted Children at Home, Hands-on Geography,* and other resource books.

Involved in local, state, and national homeschooling issues, Maggie and Bob both serve on boards of home education organizations in Delaware. They're also owners of Bright Ideas Press, publishers of The Mystery of History Series, Christian Kids Explore Science Series, and other practical, fun, and affordable materials for the homeschool market. Contact them at www.BrightIdeasPress.com or at 877-492-8081.

# The Importance of
# Seeing Ernest
## or
# The Adventure of
# Discovering the Design
# of God

### *Diana Waring*

The day Isaac rode the merry-go-round was life changing for me. As I waited impatiently, wondering why on earth my six-year-old was talking to the carnival ride operator—one of Isaac's many quirks was to talk to anyone he saw—and wondering in anger what crazy stunt he would pull next to embarrass me, Isaac's Creator stopped me in my tracks.

*"Diana! Enough! I made that boy in my image, for my plans and purposes—not yours—and you need to honor and respect him!"*

Gulp.

Words are all I have to convey the understanding God gave me that day in 1987, but mere words could never fully express the tremendous "oomph" I felt. My selfishness and self-centered pride were suddenly and clearly revealed, leaving no doubt that many of my actions toward Isaac were not motivated by godly wisdom and unselfish love for him but rather by wanting other people to think I was a good parent of a *normal* child and that I was doing an *incredible* job of homeschooling my son!

At that moment, with God's voice ringing in my heart, a fundamental, internal change occurred. I learned the importance of seeing Isaac the way God sees him. From the mountaintop clarity that that perspective brought, I slowly began to discover how to train Isaac "in the way that *he* should go."

> For You have formed my inward parts; You have covered me in my mother's womb
> I will praise You, for I am fearfully and wonderfully made;
> Marvelous are Your works, and that my soul knows very well.
> My frame was not hidden from You, when I was made in secret,
> And skillfully wrought in the lowest parts of the earth.
> Your eyes saw my substance, being yet unformed.
> And in Your book they all were written, the days fashioned for me,
> When as yet there were none of them.
> —Psalm 139:13–16 (NKJV)

The God who formed Isaac with his own marvelous and wonderful design was waiting for me to get in step with his training program.

One of the first lessons in this God-inspired program was recognizing that my six-year-old was a visual learner rather than an auditory learner like me. This lesson took several months and was played out in several sessions like this one. Observing the hurricane-proportion disaster in his room, I would march in like a drill sergeant and bark, "Isaac, make your bed; put your clothes away; pick up your books; throw away the trash; organize your toys!" Half an hour later, he would sweetly say, "I'm done, Mommy." Marching back in, I would be confronted with a bed neatly made and the rest of the disaster untouched. "Isa–a–a–a–a–ac!"

Grrr. What was wrong with him anyway? Was he too dumb to figure it out? Was he rebellious? Was he just trying to drive me crazy?

D. None of the above.

My husband, Bill, attended a weekend seminar on learning modalities (the way we best take in new information): auditory, visual, and kinesthetic. When he returned and shared the information, including a test to discover a person's learning modality, I suddenly wondered if perhaps Isaac were a visual learner, one who needed to see things written down in order to understand. I am an auditory learner, one who needs to hear it to "get it," and I assumed that everyone in the world was like me. But, if Isaac were indeed a different kind of learner, this would explain a lot.

The next day we set up a small test for Isaac (a bit of the laboratory scientist in me coming out, I suppose). Instead of barking orders at him, I handed him a short list with a place to check off each duty done.

- Make bed.
- Put clothes away.
- Pick up books.
- Throw away trash.
- Organize toys.

Half an hour later Isaac called to me, "Mommy, I'm done." To my utter astonishment, he had accomplished everything on the list, and, for the first time in his life, I had the joy of seeing a room satisfactorily cleaned by my own son.

Another aspect of this lesson was learned when my second son, Michael, memorized his multiplication tables as a nine-year-old. He was a tree-climber, room-runner, never-slow-down kind of kid, and when it came time for him to sit quietly and memorize, I almost lost my salvation.

"Michael! Will you P–L–E–A–S–E quit fidgeting and just memorize!"

Try as he might, he could only sit quietly for a few minutes before some part of his body would start tapping or stomping or wiggling again. Even if he was memorizing at that moment, he was driving me crazy. What we had here was increasing frustration for two combatants. Suddenly the information learned at that weekend seminar came back to me and gave me an idea to try something I had never seen done before. Since Michael was a mover, an obviously kinesthetic, needs-to-move-to-get-it learner, I gave him a chance to do what came naturally.

"Ummm. Mike? Would you like to try doing jumping jacks and memorizing your multiplication tables at the same time?"

In the twinkling of an eye, Michael was fully engaged in doing both room-sized jumping jacks and memorizing "two times two is four, hey!"

Ah. Not everyone is like me. That day I learned the importance of seeing Michael the way God sees him and that things improve when I cooperate with his God-designed wiggle. Lesson noted and learned, at least, on this level.

Next divinely provided lesson: When a good friend of mine (an ex-schoolteacher) taught a class on homeschooling, I jumped at the chance to attend. She spent an evening talking about the four learning styles—feeler, thinker, sensor, intuitor—and how to use this understanding in teaching children. It was intriguing to consider just where each member of my family fit within these descriptions.

The Feeler—A people person, one who cares about the people perspective, who enjoys being with people, who is subjective rather than objective. Well, that was obviously Isaac. He blossomed around people and wilted when going too long without a regular infusion of people time.

The Thinker—A "give me the facts, ma'am, just the facts" person, one who cares about the objective realities, the authoritative facts, who sees things in black-and-white. The thinker likes schedules, routines, orderliness. That was Melody, my daughter, in living color! She thrived on knowing when every assignment was due, what books were required, and who, exactly, did the lunch dishes on Thursdays.

The Sensor—A "see the hill, take the hill" person, one who is a "take charge and make it happen" kind of person, with a physical approach to life. The sensor is a mover, a fixer, a builder, a hands-on do-it-yourself-er. Michael fit this description like a glove. From his incredible dexterity preparing fabulous food, to his leather working, oil painting, and ballet, Michael showed a zest for being physically expressive.

The Intuitor—An "imagine the possibilities" person, one who excels at coming up with ideas, who daydreams a lot, who greatly enjoys the pursuit of a project but sees no reason to complete a project if it ceases being interesting. An intuitor holds no regard for routine but thrives on the spur of the moment. An intuitor is to routine as a black duck is to a red rock—there is no connection. For better or worse, that was me to a T. I was really good at coming up with great ideas for my children and really bad at bringing them to completion. Fortunately for my family, Bill excelled at helping us finish what we started. Whew!

Knowing about these learning styles did not, however, guarantee success. One has to implement the knowledge on a regular basis in order to see the blessing. I had been neglecting that when one day Isaac came to me as a sixteen-year-old and said,

"Mom, I really hate school!" Since by that time I was becoming known as a homeschool author and speaker, I felt like this put my reputation on the verge of destruction, and I got slightly worked up.

"Go ahead, Isaac, just kill me now and get it over with."

Within a few minutes, however, the realizations, first that my reputation didn't matter nearly as much as my son's love of learning and, second, that salvaging our relationship was more important than staying angry, helped me calm down and begin gently to probe his newly discovered hatred of school. With some astonishment and chagrin I heard his reasons.

"You know, Mom, ever since I reached high school age, you've handed me a pile of books and told me to go off by myself to work on them. Couldn't you do a couple of these subjects with me?"

Oh, my. I had forgotten the cardinal rule for feelers: give them sufficient people time. Once we adjusted that part of the schedule, once we added face time so he could interact with me about what he was learning, Isaac began to thrive again.

And then there was the day that ten-year-old Melody asked me, "Mom, do we have any Christmas wrapping paper?" In shock, I quickly scanned the calendar to make certain I knew what month it was.

"Melody, it's only the beginning of November. Of course we don't have any Christmas wrapping paper."

"Mom, I need Christmas wrapping paper."

Sigh. "Honey, listen, we don't need wrapping paper until Christmas Eve because we don't wrap presents till the last minute. As a matter of fact, we usually don't have presents to wrap till the last minute!"

Silence. Sudden dawning realization.

"Um, Melody, do you have Christmas presents to wrap?"

"Yes."

Aha. Despite the genetic influence of a will-o'-the-wisp, intuitor mother who usually remembered Christmas presents a few days before Christmas, my own flesh-and-blood daughter was made of different stuff, thinker stuff. So what's a mother to do? Buy the Christmas wrapping paper in November, of course. (True to life, Melody had to remind me three or four times before I finally remembered to pick it up.)

There were smiles all around the day I learned the importance of seeing Melody the way God sees her, and not only cooperating with her thinker-structured mind-set but even giving God thanks for it. Nowadays, we enjoy wrapped presents—bows and all—displayed around the living room before we ever get a tree!

The third "pay attention, this is important" lesson from God's training program was when we learned the newly formulated theory of the eight intelligences. Our divinely appointed instructor was an energetic firebrand from New Zealand named Rosalie Pedder. She taught one week at the Youth with a Mission Discipleship Training School that Bill and I attended in Auckland, New Zealand, in 1999. (Our entire family had come to New Zealand for an international mission experience, and God did far more in that trip than we had ever envisioned.)

This particular week was focused on understanding God's design in each of us as learners. Rosalie taught about the many aspects of our educational design, including the learning modalities and styles, but the information on the eight intelligences was life changing for our family. We discovered that there are ways God has made us "smart"—every person on the face of the earth! Though these are recognized and valued throughout the culture, only two are valued in traditional educational settings. We have each of these eight intelligences in a blend of strengths (i.e., some are more intelligent in math-logic, while others are more intelligent in music), and we can each grow in all of these eight intelligences. That means we are not limited to what we can do today in moving our bodies or in getting along with people, in writing articles or in observing cloud formations, in knowing our ability to handle a difficult situation or in painting landscapes, but we can grow and develop. In other words, we *are* fearfully and wonderfully made, designed with incredible care and foresight by God himself.

What are these different areas, these eight intelligences?

- Intrapersonal (self-smart)
- Naturalist (nature smart)
- Musical (music smart)
- Math-logical (number smart)
- Bodily-kinesthetic (body smart)
- Interpersonal (people smart)
- Linguistic (word smart)
- Spatial (picture smart)

Consider this: each one of us has these different intelligences, to one degree or another, as part of God's grand design for his plans and purposes for our lives. What does that mean to us as homeschooling parents? For me, first and foremost, it means that I recognize that, though my children are different from me (sometimes in ways that make me crazy), they are nevertheless equally designed by an all-wise God. That means, second, that not only do I recognize this, but I also need to respect that design—to honor and work with it as much as possible.

What does that look like in real life? Here are some examples:

Thomas Alva Edison, one of the greatest inventors of all time, went to school for only three months before his teacher said that he was "addled." His mother promptly brought him home to teach him herself. She used a method of drawing him into learning by "exploring" knowledge—doing experiments, observing phenomena, and such. He spent much of his time alone, which enabled him (in his intrapersonal intelligence) to accomplish amazing feats of discovery and invention. In fact, when questioned later in life about his refusal to have a simple surgery to correct his deafness, he responded with the fact that his deafness helped him to focus on the task at hand!

Dr. Paul Brand, the surgeon who helped lepers worldwide by discovering how to avoid the disfiguring damage caused by leprosy, was taught for several years by his missionary mother in the mountains of India. Recognizing Paul's love of nature (his naturalist intelligence), she allowed him to do his schoolwork sitting in a tree house. He would lower his work down to his mother by use of a rope and pulley, and, if the answers were right, he could stay up among the birds!

Franz Joseph Haydn, the classical composer who sought to bring rest and refreshment through his music, was born to a music-loving, God-honoring family in Austria. Seeing his musical intelligence, his parents worked with his design in the only way they understood, by sending him to Vienna for musical training when he was a young boy. His commitment to making his living as a musician/composer meant that he spent a number of years in poverty. However, in his perseverance through all of the trials, he finally gained the opportunity to compose full-time for Prince Esterhazy. This resulted in a tremendous amount of beautiful music, and the world is richer (and more refreshed!) for it.

Louis Pasteur, the scientist who discovered how to prevent death by rabies, how to prevent infection after surgery, how to save the silkworm industry in France, how to keep chickens from dying of chicken cholera and sheep from dying of anthrax, as well as saving the wine crop of France in 1864 by pasteurization, was considered in elementary school to be a slow student. Louis was someone who used logic (the math-logical intelligence) to discover answers to seemingly impossible problems. At his moment of history, many scientists believed in the theory of spontaneous generation, that life often sprang spontaneously out of nothing, as evidenced in maggots arising "spontaneously" out of rotted meat. Pasteur used logical experiments to disprove this theory, experiments that have never been thrown out.

Jim Thorpe, arguably the best all-around athlete in the world, was a Native American who won Olympic gold for the United States. As a boy he loved to run and track game in the woods around his father's farm in Oklahoma, and his athletic talents were further developed at the Carlisle Indian Industrial School in Pennsylvania. His teachers recognized his amazing gifts and encouraged him to try a variety of sports and athletic activities. His bodily-kinesthetic intelligence was displayed for the entire world at the 1912 Olympic Games in Sweden when he became the first man ever to win both the pentathlon and decathlon. His versatility in all sports was evident when he became both a professional baseball player for six years and then a professional football player for fifteen years!

Mary Slessor, the Scottish missionary to Africa, had a marvelous ability to work with people (the interpersonal intelligence). As a young Christian woman, she volunteered to do home missions in a dangerous area of Dundee, Scotland, where gangs ran rampant. Mary was not only able to stand up to their threats; she was able to convince them to come to her Sunday school class, where the biggest bully of all was converted the first day! This God-given intelligence, as well as her experiences in Scotland, prepared her to face African warriors with courage and justice. Her abilities were noted by the British government, and, in recognition of this, she was made vice-consul of the Okoyong region of Nigeria, the first woman ever to hold this position in the British Empire, where she settled disputes over land, money, and broken relationships.

Clive Staples (C. S.) Lewis, one of the most influential Christian writers and apologists of the last century, was immersed in languages early in life. His mother, before she died, taught him French and Latin as well as a love for reading. His whole world as a child seemed to revolve around reading, writing, and imagining. When he was sent to boarding school, he devoured literature like others devour meat! His eventual studies at Oxford were in medieval literature, of which he was an acknowledged master. It was due to his linguistic intelligence that Lewis was able to write such beloved literature as The Chronicles of Narnia, *The Pilgrim's Regress*, and *The Screwtape Letters*.

Jan Van Eyck, the most famous painter of Northern Europe during the 1400s, was the first painter to create the sense that one was looking through an open window or door into a room, as well as the first painter to master oil paints, which allowed for the possibility of rich, velvety colors in the paint. Van Eyck's spatial intelligence can be clearly seen in one of his most famous paintings, *The Annunciation*. He creates an amazing perspective, looking into the interior of a church as the angel Gabriel makes his profound announcement to Mary. Not only do we see vivid colors in tremendous detail, but we are also treated to a complex visual picture of this utterly significant moment in history.

All of these intelligences are part of our warp and woof, our God-given design for his plans and purposes. As homeschooling parents, we need to be set free from the "one size fits all" mentality that we experienced in school, and we need to allow our children space and grace as they try out these different areas in everyday life, discovering their unique blend of strengths and weaknesses. That may mean letting our children do some of their schoolwork outside or allowing them to present what they have learned by doing an art project. It may mean giving them a tape recorder in order to capture their storytelling or giving them time alone to work on a project. Perhaps our children need music lessons, or lively reading books, or cooperative learning with friends, or bicycle time.

This is where the adventure comes in! Imagine yourself setting off on a treasure hunt with your family, knowing that the path will become clearer as you watch for and interpret clues along the way. Think of the delight of ongoing discovery as your family's journey results in young people who love learning and who eventually find great fulfillment and satisfaction in doing what they were created to do. That's why it is critical for us to learn "the importance of seeing Ernest"!

※   ※   ※

Diana Waring, with her husband Bill, has ministered to homeschooling families on four continents. Her expertise comes through mentoring by a pro-homeschooling international Christian educator, listening to other veterans, asking lots of questions, personal experience (her three children—from 1985 until the youngest graduated in 2003), and an ongoing study of biblical education from the Word of God. Contact her at www.dianawaring.com.

# Unschooling or Delight Directed Studies

*Through wisdom is a house built;*
*And by understanding it is established;*
*By knowledge the rooms are filled*
*With all precious and pleasant treasures.*

—PROVERBS 24:3–4 NKJV

❊ ❊ ❊

*I'm as impressed as the next person is when an eleven*
*year old can do calculus and is learning to think logi-*
*cally. But a kid who is reading about Robinson*
*Crusoe is thinking logically, too. It's not completely*
*different.*

—BILL GATES

If one were to lay out various methods of homeschooling on a spectrum, the traditional textbook method is often seen as the most school based, while another, more relaxed method known as unschooling or delight-directed learning would be the antithesis of the stereotypical school experience. Unschooling turns parents into facilitators rather than teachers, per se. John Holt, a schoolteacher, originally used the term *unschooling* during the 1960s and 1970s to describe the process of learning without going to school. Since then, unschooling has been defined in various ways and is as different as each homeschool family that practices the method. Rather than incorporating the traditional school methods into the home, the unschool family creates a learning environment focused on the interests of the children being educated. Some parents removing children from the traditional school system will engage in a period of deschooling, where the focus is taken off the negatives of the school environment and placed instead on being able to relax and enjoy learning again.

While some unschoolers choose to impose little to no structure on the children, others allow the students to make some of the decisions with input and guidance from the parents. Some will establish a flexible schedule, to be molded and shaped as time and interests dictate, while others will adamantly refuse advance educational planning. In some cases textbooks will be used by the child completely against the preferences of the parent, but some parents will integrate textbooks, living books, and other resources in a manner similar to the eclectic homeschool family. The common bond between unschoolers, however, is an acknowledgement that children are able to gain valuable educational experiences from a variety of activities and resources and that the parent will create an environment rich in opportunities to learn. By encouraging children to proceed at their own pace through interests and hobbies they feel led to pursue, we can teach them to stretch their minds and solve problems as they encounter them. An inherent trust that a child will pursue a beloved topic until they have covered many core academic subjects is vital to feeling confident as an unschooling parent. Allowing children to delve into what delights and intrigues them shows them our understanding of (and confidence in) their innate ability to learn. We can demonstrate to them our own love of learning, model to them the life skills necessary to find information and search out the resources needed for our own intellectual pursuits, and instill in them a lifelong ability to gain knowledge when and where it is needed.

Whether the unschooling family chooses to create a more scheduled learning environment such as that presented by Dr. Raymond Moore and the late Dorothy Moore (known to many as the "grandparents of homeschooling") or a more relaxed environment as described by Dr. Mary Hood, the common bond is recognizing the creativity children will use to learn what they love. Join the Moores as they describe their family and professional experiences with children who have been encouraged to delight in seeking, and soaking up, what they love. Learn from Mary Hood as she describes the joys and potential pitfalls of creating a relaxed homeschool. Most of all, remember that our job as homeschoolers is to find the method that works for each child. Delaying formal academics for a few years as the Moores advocate, or choosing to focus primarily on skills and habits and letting formal learning come and go as it will, may well be what keeps a love of learning burning in your child.

# Delight Directed Studies

## *Dorothy Moore*

Raymond and I were not concerned about formal schooling until ages eight or ten or later. I already had enough experience with early school entrants in my years as a public school remedial teacher to warn me that children, especially boys, were not really ready for ongoing school at least until then. Certain that Dennis at age eight was as bright as any boy, I dutifully started on some basic skills to go with the experiences we had for an hour or so a day and let him do some work alone. He did well, covering three grades in two years.

However, he was not at all eager, and in recent years we have agreed that he might have been more highly motivated if he had waited at least another year. He didn't really take off academically until junior high, the level that researchers from Berkeley and Stanford to Columbia and Cornell say is optimal and our research thoroughly substantiates. Dennis later became covaledictorian in a large school.

In Japan, by the time Kathie was six and a half, I had gathered six other English-speaking children whose mothers pled with me to take over their education. I let Kathie sit in with them, doing her fun things. I made no attempt to teach her formally, but she surely listened. We never knew for sure how she picked up so much. We had school only in the mornings, yet she was up with the other beginners. I taught her until age nine and Dennis, thirteen—very late in those days.

## What I Learned

Knowing what I do now, though, I would work with the children even more informally. This doesn't mean I didn't require obedience; they behaved better than most. We had fun, and the children were well prepared for highly rated schools when they returned to the States. Now I wish I had continued teaching my own at home much longer than I did. Secondary school is easy. Though my philosophy, goals, and resources would stay essentially the same, I would use more projects. They are natural, realistic, and practical for children of all ages and abilities.

I took three summer classes at UCLA between my junior and senior years in college, one taught by the curriculum coordinator of Los Angeles County Public Schools. She strongly recommended the unit or project method for teaching social studies. We integrated skills such as math, reading, writing, and spelling as much as possible into the unit of study. We observed classrooms taught this way.

I launched out on a harbors project in my first classroom of second and third graders. In our well-to-do school district, we were not limited in equipment opportunities. We secured soft wood scrap at the lumberyard; purchased simple carpenter tools, nails, and paint to make little toy boats; and set up a simulated harbor in our classroom. Besides our hands-on experiences, we learned about the different kinds of boats and ships and their functions, drew pictures, read stories and books, wrote stories, sang songs, talked, and learned how to spell words about boats.

Our closing activity was a field trip to the harbor. We integrated language arts, music, art, geography, cultures, weather, and science into this theme study.

Later our unit was on early California with its early Indians, and then the padres, which incorporated Spanish architecture, geography, topography, history, vegetation, religion, food, and art. In a classroom corner, we constructed a simply furnished, early California house big enough for the children to play in. We painted a background mural of eucalyptus trees that came from Australia and are now all over California, and a Spanish mission compound so common in old California and Mexico. These social studies subjects allowed integration of many skills, including oral and written language, music, and art.

I was really too naive to understand what I now know about standardized testing, teaching to the test, or even to realize that the children's achievement is also a test of the teacher's skill. When the school routinely tested the children at the end of the school year, their scores were compared to the previous year's scores and other equivalent grades. The results showed that my children excelled in the basics, especially reading! Of course, we had been fairly consistent in working on the skills needed. Yet we had spent a lot of time with our projects, integrating as much as possible of the other subjects. That first year's record started me in remedial reading with a special class the very next year!

## How I Would Begin Homeschooling

If I had several children to teach at home, I would first work on my household routine, fitting my program into our daily needs. If my husband left for work at 7:30 a.m., I would have my children in bed early enough each night to get up at least by 6:30 to have a short worship or other family-togetherness time and breakfast with their daddy to start the day.

Next would be household chores with each one having duties to get the house in reasonable order before school. Yet I would try to work daily with my children to teach them how to do their jobs and to help them understand teamwork. For example, if my child were just learning to make his bed, I would have him help me make mine, and then I would help him make his. If I had several children, I would also train any older or more able child to help a younger or less able one (in household as well as school tasks) while we all worked toward our common goal. Cross-age and family-team education are crucial.

Then I would have school at a regular time each day, perhaps 9:00 a.m., with brief opening exercises, probably including the Pledge of Allegiance to my country's flag, a song, and, in our home, a prayer. One reason for the regular time is that it makes you and your children systematic. They are secure in knowing what's next and that mom is giving her time exclusively to them, at least for a short while. It will also help them feel that it is a real school in terms of social pressure from their friends. If under legal pressure, you can honestly report a schedule of your daily activities yet stay relaxed, informal.

## Under Eights

If most of the children were seven or under, my school would be informal, and I would try to adapt even to the youngest ones, at least for the first part. I would probably read to them, knowing that children who like to be read to will eventually learn to read; I would do some Scripture memory or other inspiring memory work and sing some songs. Since children's songs often are repetitious with simple melodies, we might think up some different words to the songs or make up songs of our own. We might do some finger plays that rhyme and perhaps invent some new ones. I might either play the piano or play some music so that the children could march around the room. I could even have some little homemade rhythm band instruments for them to keep time with the music.

In my reading I would concentrate on Bible and nature books or other character-building reading, including simple biographies of children in other lands, and the like, but always with the standards of Philippians 4:8 to be sure they are true, honest, just, pure, lovely, and of good report. There are several reasons for this. Young children do not distinguish well between reality and fantasy and can become confused. For example, the story of Santa Claus is fantasy, but the stories describe him with many of the same qualities as Christ. When children eventually find out that Santa Claus is a myth, some may believe that Christ is a myth, too. In addition, true books teach truth at the same time they entertain. They often are a help not only in teaching integrity but also in building other sound character qualities.

While my hands were busy with household duties, I would ask the children to work with me, not worrying about their ineptness. I would tell them family stories, let them talk, answer questions, expressing appreciation for their help, and mother them naturally. Such warm educationally responsive time with children is Smithsonian's first ingredient in its recipe for genius. I would also try to include others important to my children to share in the delightful activity of reading aloud to them.

My brother visited us in Japan while he was U.S. Army Inspector General in Korea. Soon our three-year-old Kathie brought her favorite book, climbed on his lap, and asked him to read to her. After his initial shock, he did. Dennis, a little shyer, would sit beside whatever visitor Kathie fascinated. One time it was Japan's Senior Prince Takamatsu, the emperor's brother!

As I noted their interests and need to express themselves, we would stop occasionally to talk about the pictures in the book or discuss their questions. Often I would read stories that have tiny pictures interspersed instead of key words and let each child have a turn reading the pictures. I might have the older child read some words or parts of the story, as he is able. I would call attention to the title of the book or story and key words that may be repeated often, such as the main characters.

Because they usually watched the book I was reading, I sometimes moved my finger from left to right to show how the words progress left to right across the page. This is a learned technique. Nothing in our brain is built-in to tell us that. Old Hebrew writing was from right to left, and Japanese kanji may be vertical, horizontal, right to left, or left to right, depending on its use (hymnal, book, etc.). It is normal for a young child to reverse letters and words in his first efforts to write: *was* becomes *saw*. If the direction taken by words is not learned in the early steps of reading, a bad habit of reversals may be hard to over-come. Yet this is not dyslexia! Dyslexia as commonly applied to anyone who cannot read is technically incorrect, though reversal may be a symptom of a truly dyslexic child.

It is important to adjust the length and variety of that first school session to the ages, needs, and attention spans of the children. Young children do best with short, quiet periods inter-spersed with work or play activity—recess. If the weather is bad, marching, hopping, tiptoeing, and even fun calisthenics to music add variety for physical education.

A little later I would involve them in a project. Perhaps we would go grocery shopping where they helped identify different items by their labels. They might make lists with pictures if not with words. Food preparation with measuring, gardening, nature study, a visit to a shut-in, or making greeting cards or mementos for relatives or friends are other great hands-on projects. I would dictate the spelling of some words for the one who knows his letters and help the others copy or even trace over my model of the message they wanted to convey.

More often than not, there might be other activities I prom-
ised "when we have time." Such activities might include digging
up ants to make an ant farm, perhaps hunting for the queen ant
(without getting bitten!); doing a simple experiment we read
about in a children's magazine or book; going to the library or
possibly finding some information in our encyclopedia about
a praying mantis that the children found yesterday. You are, in a
sense, always teaching but relaxed in doing so.

If my six- or seven-year-old or younger were eager to learn
to read or write, I might spend an extra five to ten minutes a
day or even twice a day with him in informal instruction and
limit his reading time to fifteen to thirty minutes at a time,
depending on his age. That instruction would include simple
phonics and reading, including reading aloud together if he
had progressed that far, and writing or a simple math game.
Pennsylvania psychiatrist and reading author Robert McKay has
often suggested that we stress this togetherness in reading and
singing. You will not want to ignore your younger ones if they
want to listen in, too.

I would carefully note how much my child really wanted
these things, asking myself, *Am I pushing this on him?* Some discover that reading doesn't come automatically, and your child
may lose interest for a while. Be sensitive to this so as not to
pressure him and spoil his long-term motivation for learning.

I also watched for opportunities that arose during the day
that might serve as a springboard for our next morning session.
I would also be alert to use counting and measuring for math and
any other time that could become a teachable moment, such as
meal preparation for teaching nutrition and health.

Our kitchen lent itself to simple science experiments. For
example, we studied the uses of yeast and found reason to be
careful about uses of some baking powders and soda, vinegar,
and such. We experimented as well with taste, touch, and smell.

We "discovered" creatures, flowers, or plants in our yard or on our walks. Simple map study, directions, and general layout in our neighborhood and community became our social studies. Occasional experiences that the children dictated for their "own book" was creative writing.

Now what essential subject did I miss? None. These are only a sample of the basic learning that goes on naturally within the four walls and neighborhood of a home. Don't forget manners, honesty, promptness, dependability, practical arts, common sense, and compassion. I would do this program not only because it is good preschool education for my children, but in order to have a daily log of activities in case I needed it in my state as proof that my six-year-old is indeed being educated. However, be careful! An overanxious mother can adopt too much of a teaching mode even with this program, pushing her children into formal ideas of what they should learn instead of being sensitive to their readiness and interests.

## After Seven or Eight

Depending on the children's needs, ages, and maturity (including secondary students, who are ready for some formal work in skills), we may spend twenty minutes to an hour in practice, drill, and even simple workbooks, for mastery is our goal. As the project study unfolds, and spelling, math, and reading are tools to explore the subject of interest, however, these skills become more relevant and practical. Many boys are reluctant penmen, even up to ten, eleven, or even later. Five or ten minutes a day of consistent practice might be enough. If they are writing to an important person like a governor, head of the church, or a pen pal, the minutes go faster. Use their interests!

I would train my children to be as obedient and independent of my help as is reasonable for their ages. I would also face the fact that if I had any children under the age of four or five, I could reasonably expect that they would interrupt me because they needed attention. My schedule won't go smoothly every day. I can't do all the nice things with or without my children that I would like to do. I also can't have the social life or do what I see other mothers do who send all their children to school.

## How a Unit of Study Works

The rest of the morning, I would spend on project (or unit or theme) learning, starting with any of the content subjects, that is, science, social studies, religion. Explore, first on your own, then with your children, activities that help to integrate the skills and other content subjects into your main topic.

As a Christian, the Bible would be my first choice for its wide range of study, including both skills and other content subjects: language arts; some math; some science; geography; history; economics; government; music; arts and crafts; and best of all, the related character qualities developed in the study of Bible heroes and events.

Yet by repeating only the facts of sacred happenings without developing a deeper understanding and application of the lessons inherent in the examples given, spiritual study becomes as dull and lifeless as workbooks. Combine your experience with their ideas; devise activities that make stories real; talk about whys and hows—the exciting motives and God's purpose in each study and what lessons we can learn from the study.

Are your youngsters interested in specific wars or explorers? Include the wars of the ages and kings like Xerxes, queens like Esther, and cities like Susa (Shushan) and Babylon in your studies. Start with one idea and let it grow with your own and your children's inventions. It's like winding up a ball of cord or starting with a small, tightly packed snowball and rolling it in the snow. They just keep growing. Remember: Things learned by experience last longer, and concepts, attitudes, values, and creativity are lifelong while facts may be temporary, especially if neither reviewed nor often used.

Initially, if your children have been in traditional school, they may be at a loss for any ideas of their own. You may have to start gradually to resurrect and redevelop their creativity. It takes some families several months and some a year or two for this to happen. Allow yourself and your children a little time for creative thought, and ideas will come.

Your job as teacher is not just to communicate knowledge but to impart that vitalizing energy which is inherent in the mind-to-mind and heart-to-heart relationship of one-to-one teaching. You will be most successful if you continue to use mothering and fathering methods instead of trying to be a typical classroom teacher. Who taught your children to walk, talk, and know their colors? Who taught your children how to count and do many other skills? You didn't force this learning. They were eager to learn when they were ready, but you were there to encourage with your help and warm responses. Try to maintain this wonderful motivation of early childhood, and you will have a happy, low-stress experience in homeschool.

Dorothy Moore was born in Bruce, South Dakota. She married Raymond Moore in June 1938. Together they have two children and seven chosen children. She has authored or coauthored thirteen books and several manuals. She served as editor of the *Moore Report International,* teacher, lecturer, consultant and faculty at several universities, private schools, and colleges. Sheis sometimes called the cofounder and "grand-mother" of the modern homeschool movement.

During her life Dorothy was recognized for her many accomplishments and honors, but none were more special to her than her marriageto Raymond and her motherhood to their children. Dorothy went home to be with the Lord in 2002.

# The Moore Formula

## Raymond Moore

I believe you will be much more likely to learn what the editors assigned me to write and be more highly motivated to get into the fine material in this chapter if we give you a hint of how homeschool movement founders made their way through some pretty rough places to great discoveries. Few homeschool parents know the story except pioneers of twenty-five to forty years ago. This is the first time a few Moore Formula secrets are published as a blend of research, analysis, world-class scholarship writings, experimentation, inspired writers, and Scripture. Dorothy and I uncovered what was to us a dazzling spectrum of teaching secrets for both homes and classrooms.

Our seminars once centered on homeschools. Now we target all schools—public, private, and parochial, mostly using home-schools as our models. They derive from Scripture (Mal. 4:5–6), inspired writings, sound research, and highly successful experiments from North America to Uganda, and Fiji to Japan. Old America showed homeschools at their highest and best, from colonial days through the Industrial Revolution. Our goal now, as you will shortly see, is to upgrade parents and teachers in family values, peer influence, manual skills, the brain, senses, cognition, and others. For example, in cognition we show how students can, by age twelve, reach adult reasonability as Christ did—an immense boon in behavior and learning as they deal maturely with whys and hows.

I am no theologian but a plain teacher, trained widely and deeply in child development and university administration. I did not need nor did I deserve special honors. God is the one to be honored. It did help, however, to have worked in many ways with students. The list may bore you. I have been a teacher, principal, city school superintendent, college dean and president, university vice president, dean of teacher education, U.S. Office of Education, U.S. Representative to UNESCO, director of an international university consortium (Chicago, Johns Hopkins, Southern Illinois, Stanford, Tulane, and Wisconsin), and a director of research for early childhood projects at Colorado, Stanford, and Southern California.

Yet most importantly, humanly speaking, I was married nearly sixty-four years to a master teacher who even in death shares her writings with me in this manuscript. We avoided derision of conventional schools and shared our methods with them. School officials and teachers must deal with complex tasks and dark influences these days. Let's love them as we used to wish they would love us!

You will shortly understand why Dorothy remains the heroine of many of us. Her share in the Moore Formula is a unique vineyard whose vine slips have been grafted worldwide, its flavor as nourishing as it is sweet.

## The Miraculous Synergy of Study with Work

The merging of work with study has a synergic effect of providing much more than double the brainpower, in addition to the finest form of discipline, skills, and self-control. You will see this in some of our stories. Judged this way, you will soon sense that without being teacher guided the average school is a one-handled wheelbarrow. In homes and schools that add the other handle, working with parent or teacher, brainpower is not added but multiplied. With it also comes the friendly discipline of discipleship, and self-control.

Tradition first demands academic proficiency in such areas as reading, math, spelling, and languages. We do not ignore these, but in the Moore Formula we stress manual skills as at least as important as academics. When in your hand the tender clay of your youngsters touches a potter's wheel, the Moore Formula sets out to mold balanced and worthy teachers and students to become their warm and selfless best. We have never had it fail, given a heart full of what Moses called "diligence," the blessings of God, and common sense (Deut. 28:1–13).

In quietness and confidence, such students find their strength. Simplicity and diligence provide the richest of classics and culture. Gentleness, kindness, cooperation, and manners warmly share the golden rule, and peer dependence retires. The apostle Paul blends, fuses, and harmonizes this in Philippians 4:8: "Finally, . . . whatsoever things are true, . . . honest, . . . just, . . . pure, . . . lovely, . . . of good report, if there be any virtue, and if there be any praise, think on these things."

## The Makings of Superb Teaching

In brief, to be a great teacher depends more on how kindly, selflessly, and thoughtfully you live than on how much you know. That ideal will visit you and your children dressed in its best both at home and in school. We put this all into a model in 1947–51 when I was graduate dean and head of teacher education at Pacific Union College, a highly rated small college at the head of California's Napa Valley. We gave a copy of the book

*Education* and brief précis each to Chairman John Michaelis, Cal-Berkeley educational sociologist, and each member of the state accrediting team, including the presidents of a well-known Oakland woman's college and a major Roman Catholic college.

What do you really want from a school? A diploma? New friends? Excitement? Individual attention? Cultural advantages? Classical nuances? Manual skills? Creative mastery? A strong record of warm time-wait responsiveness? Physical, mental, and spiritual safety? Character? Self-control? How and where would you start looking in today's market for executives, scholars, scientists, or top-drawer homemakers, businessmen, and skilled workers of sterling character who offer the promise of industrial or professional crown princes, leadership models for a new age? Please think as you read on.

## Moore Formula Heroes and Heroines

Here we give you a couple of examples of families who followed the Moore Formula they learned from Moore seminars, television, radio, or the Moore Academy. One family had its own program but used the same methods.

### MARSH, OXFORD RESEARCH PROFESSOR

Cheryl Marsh unknowingly brought us another record-setter when she called our office, worried that her six-year-old Barnaby already disliked studying his (formal) lessons. He was preoccupied with "fixing hurt birds" in Alaska's Denali wilderness. Dorothy and her lead teacher, Ellen Dana, told Mrs. Marsh not to worry; just give him all the good bird books they can find, including simple healing materials and methods, and special books on writing. Be alert for bird watchers and ornithologists. Accommodate his interests, aptitudes, and abilities. Watch his studies skyrocket. She did. And he did.

They knew that with such sharp motivation, academics would soon fall into line. Before long Barnaby was writing for ornithological journals and other publications. Harvard awarded him an all-expense scholarship. After a year he accepted a similar grant from Cornell with its superior ornithology program. Similarly Oxford University offered a scholarship and wanted to keep him. Cornell, however, said no. After returning to Cornell for graduation, Barnaby accepted a Rhodes Scholarship and finished his doctorate at Oxford. He spent three summers as a Smithsonian intern, and Barnaby is now on the Oxford faculty.

### HARRINGTONS

The Harrington kids caught the homeschool fever after Kevin and Kirstin read our *Harper's-Reader's Digest* report on early schooling. Kirstin is a mom who also writes in the *Successful Homeschool Family Handbook* that her obsession with formal studies at first stifled any faith in the Moore Formula. So she turned her job as head teacher over to Kevin, who is still teaching their youngest at home.

Kirstin recalls with pride the results. They were a family of two devoted parents and eleven kids in Idaho, where for years the state threatened jail for parents who taught their kids at home. They experimented briefly with public and church schools but settled on the Moore Formula because of their concern for family values. They illustrate well how the Formula works with an impoverished family.

They thrived as the family gathered round a daily tofu/sprouts industry that supplied Boise supermarkets and learned the meaning of manual labor, side by side with mom and dad. Always when I asked one of them how they all did so well in their studies, they were quick to add, like the Colfaxes, that "when we finished our work, we couldn't wait to study." Their models were home-educated kids like George Washington,

Abraham Lincoln, Thomas Edison, George Washington Carver, and Christ. Although all are devoted to science or medicine, their parents specialized in neither.

For this book we will take Joe, who was four foot ten at age thirteen, as our example. Before his tardy adolescent growth spurt, Joe set out to teach Simplot Corporation, Idaho's chemical, ethanol, gold-refining and potato-producing giant, how to improve its gold-refining profits. His story includes most of the operational features of the Moore Formula and its solutions for homeschool problems.

For at least half of every day, Joe helped his family produce and market tofu and sprouts during his work-education hours to balance study time; this sometimes ran over half of the day. Meanwhile Joe's five older homeschooled siblings, led by his sisters who had also been his tofu-sprout mentors, were already on all-expense university scholarships at Stanford, Idaho, Southern California, and Loma Linda University Medical School (LLU), four of them in medicine and one in space physics on a National Science Foundation fellowship at Stanford.

Like Tom Edison, Joe had a dream. His dad gave him a science book that turned his devotion from tofu and sprouts (their family livelihood) to tiny bacteria and gave him exciting ideas. This fit well the Moore Formula philosophy, goals, methods, and resources. Given freedom to accommodate his initiative and creativity, Joe phoned Simplot's chief engineer, two vice presidents, and a University of Idaho (UI) professor who knew something about gold refining, so officials graciously escorted him through their plant.

When at the tour's end, his hosts asked him if he had any questions. He said, "Yes. Have you ever thought of using bacteria to isolate your gold from the ore?" The officials shook their heads, no. They invited him to put his ideas on paper and keep track of his expenses. A few days and a birthday later, Joe delivered his report and a bill for $196.80. They shortly offered him a $10,000 contract for more details and later, still another $10,000. Several years later Simplot was investing over $125,000 yearly in Joe, his ideas, and his helper—his brother James.

Meanwhile, he was working toward a metallurgical engineering master's degree on a Goldwater Scholarship at UI, and his brother, James, on an M.A. in microbiology, when executives asked Joe to be Simplot's research-grant liaison with the university. By the time he was turning twenty, they asked him to direct development of a new gold-refining plant, which dipped his bacteria rainbow into a pot of gold—300-percent more gold per ton of ore at an operating increase of only 40 percent. Joe went on to win the UI Metallurgy Prize. Now at twenty-eight, after five years as head of his Greenworld Science Inc., he had contracts with Simplot and U.S. FORTUNE-500 and overseas industrial giants, among other things, to remove impurities from factory effluents. With bacteria, of course, and a seven-figure income.

At this writing, Joe is still too busy to move ahead with his $200,000 M.D.-Ph.D. grant at LLUMS where his sister Kristin graduated before doing her psychiatry fellowship at USC, and sister Katy and brother John led their classes on identical $200,000 scholarships. Katy's twin, Kevin Jr., is into space physics at Stanford where for six years he has been on a National Science Foundation grant, and Dan indulges in UI math while servicing computer-consulting contracts with a range of corporations. Sylvia was the family's second mother, with scant interest in college until she turned eighteen, when to everyone's surprise she caught the family contagion. Within a year she was leading Nebraska's Union College in math, held an assistantship in chemistry, and had determined to be "a woman's doctor." No Harrington can any longer remotely be classified as living in poverty.

The Moore Formula is Creator-designed therapy from Scripture, research, and authors he inspired. Among those appraising its principles and methods as superior are scholars from such universities as Cal-Berkeley, Columbia, Cornell, Johns-Hopkins, and Stanford. Let's try a broad perspective of the Formula, including the work and service elements where I shared with Dorothy. It accentuates among other things:

1. Readiness—mentally, physically, socially, and spiritually as we have formulated at all levels over the last sixty-five years.

2. Creative freedom for the student (in contrast with most formal education) as proven by the Smithsonian study on genius, by the noted *Eight-Year Study* of the Carnegie Foundation, and by our experience as teachers, teacher educators, researchers, and administrators in public, private, church, and government offices and institutions.

3. Student interests as a high priority, with instant motivation flowing from them to make sound learning a delight.

4. Student aptitudes and abilities, ensuring that they, along with interests, are weighed in terms of high character development.

5. Health—mentally, physically, spiritually, and socially based essentially on the apostle Paul's master teaching in his letters to the Corinthians (1 Cor. 10:31 NKJV): "Therefore, whether you eat or drink, or whatever you do, do all to the glory of God."

6. Work-study-service balance of manual skills and studies to maximize the development of head, hands, heart, and health. At least half of the time, there should be hands-on work jointly with parents or teachers; adults sharing authority commensurate with kids' accountability.

7. Self-teaching and teacher-friendly materials instead of requiring all children to digest the same books regardless of individual differences.

8. Home industry balanced with home and community service.

9. Abundant freedom to explore.

10. Generous *time-wait* and warm adult responses with little or no rote homework. Homework should be work at home!

The Formula includes moral and scientific counsel on lifestyle and manners that authorities like William Bennett, James Dobson, and Phyllis Schlafly credit as world leading. For years it has been friendly with pioneering magazines like *Home Education, The Link,* and *The Old Schoolhouse* in the West and *Family Times* and *Growing without Schooling* in the East—all journals that sacrifice financially if necessary by serving all worthy methods and faiths.

## The Motorcycle Boy or How to Do a Project or Teach a Unit

I think her name was Conchita Delacruz, but we are not sure. We often called her "the lady from Houston." She called us one morning from Texas, and I took the phone because Dorothy and the teacher whose turn it was that week to be our noontime receptionist were both on the phone. Most of our teaching staff was out to lunch. Dorothy joined me shortly.

Conchita's tearful voice and an occasional sob suggested trouble on the horizon. She said her ten-year-old boy was withdrawing. He would seldom talk with anyone and would hardly eat. Because of some things he was saying, she suspected he could be suicidal.

"Is he in school?" we asked.

"In the fourth grade—very bright but doing very badly."

"When did he start school?"

"He was almost five."

We knew instantly that his early school entrance had given him a bad start, and he likely had never caught up. This happens with thirteen boys to every girl, for boys mature later than girls do. Very bright but never had a chance. School was a prison.

"What are his interests?" I asked.

"That's the trouble—not an interest in the world!"

"That's impossible," we protested.

Dorothy added, "A boy with no interests would have to be in the grave."

"Oh, no! He's not in the grave!" she replied. "He sleeps and eats and lives motorcycles!" To Conchita, this was totally unacceptable as a worthy interest.

"Take him out of school immediately," I advised. Normally we would have waited until the next long vacation, but this was an emergency. "Then take him to the best magazine stand in town. Let him buy his favorite motorcycle magazine and watch his reaction. Go to the library, if you can, and let him look up motorcycles in an encyclopedia. World Book usually has a spread in color."

Three months later Conchita called. She had been diligent as Dorothy and our ladies had specified when they told her how to set up a unit of study for Ramon (who was nicknamed Jimmy). They called it "transportation," including not only motorcycles but also everything that rolls, walks, floats, flies, and much more. The idea was to make the most of her son's interest by broadening it gradually to take in all the skills and learning normally expected of a boy his age. Only by using his interests, he would learn much more and many times faster. His learning would expand.

"I am so grateful," she said, this time again with tears in her voice but for a different reason, "Ramon is so excited about homeschool. He's into bicycles, cars, trucks, planes, boats, and everything in between. He's discovered that motorcycles aren't the only things on wheels. He's into jin-rickshas in Japan, carabao carts in the Philippines, camels in the Middle East, and 747 jets in Seattle. He knows more about geography than all the kids around here put together do. He knows races, faiths, and cultures like I never had any idea he would know. He is also into all kinds of math—distances and costs, used car costs, repairs, even depreciation. Of course, he is into internal combustion motors with all the chemistry and physics in them. Thank you, thank you!

"Oh, and also," Conchita continued, "Ramon works down at a local lawn mower shop where he does cleanup and is errand boy. No pay, except for an occasional extra on his bicycle, and lots of teaching by mechanics about fixing motors. He's not yet thinking about college, but he'll make a great mechanic. Our aged or ill neighbors just love him!" We, of course, were delighted.

## Cross-age Teaching

We recommend cross-age teaching for home or school while using the Moore Formula principles and methods. We have never seen it fail if diligently applied. Both teachers and students in home or in school become better learners and time managers. It is as old as the hills as a homeschool method.

## Research on Readiness

The Moore Formula places a high value on student readiness that avoids peer dependence, loss of family values, and damage to the senses. It helps individual student interests, aptitudes, and abilities that flower in a balance of study, work, and service. Extra learning power dawns with much greater freedom to develop initiative, leadership, and creativity. It not only exudes the discipline of discipleship, it teaches students the skills of the master; learning how to earn a living as well as shoot a basket, swing a bat, or kick a ball. It also brings early cognitive maturity that understands the whys and hows.

## The Marvel of Early Cognition

A University of Oklahoma study adds a happy dimension to the Smithsonian recipe for genius and to Jean Piaget's measure of reasonability. Children who grow up close to warm and responsive parents may achieve adult-level cognition by ages eight to twelve instead of waiting for fifteen to twenty, Piaget's average for Americans. Such early perception opens wide the gates to rapid learning, maturity, creativity, and discipline—like Jesus, who out-reasoned the rabbis by age twelve instead of waiting four to twelve years for maturity.

Tots whose readiness is violated or overlooked today will suffer tomorrow. Such parents remind me of a child I saw trying to tickle a polliwog into hopping before he dropped his tail. A society that strait-jackets youngsters into institutional life years before they are ready, places them at risk in a violent culture with fading values born of immaturity, often fatherless, frequently born out of wedlock, deprived by divorce, latent hardships which are often worse than deprivation by death. Yet we institution-alize them with alacrity.

## The Senses and Other Learning Media

When we analyzed the maturity of such learning means as vision, hearing, intersensory perception, brain development, cog-nition, and sociability, uncommon "coincidences" emerged. In every sense or other learning mode, readiness settled within the age-range of ten to fourteen—at about junior high school ages. So say scholars from Cal-Berkeley, Columbia, Cornell, Princeton,

Stanford, and Southern California. We call this the "integrated maturity level" or IML. Our revision of *School Can Wait II* offers 756 supporting studies out of thousands we analyzed. It cites research to showing the senses—hearing, vision, taste, touch, brain development, cognition, and even social abilities—of the young child under eight or ten are not ready for school and school tasks without damage to their immature bodies and minds.

Because auditory discrimination (ability to hear the fine joint-nuances of reason and hearing) is not yet mature, we often hear tots say *retarded* instead of *retired* and *fat* foods in place of *fast* foods. Students leave their classes with different ideas than teachers intend!

Try a true-to-life story about five-year-old Jimmy's appraisal of a retirement center. I can vouch for the picture but especially want you to note how a young child, yet immature in both hearing acuity and lifestyles of grandpas and grandmas, interprets the scene. This is what the average parent and teacher, who does not understand how immaturity of cognition and senses often reacts, is up against.

It was after a Christmas break from kindergarten when the teacher asked her brood how they spent their holidays. This was Jimmy's report:

> We always spend Christmas with Grampa 'n Gramma. They used to live up here in a big red brick house, but Grampa got retarded and they moved to Florida. They live in tin huts with a lot of retarded people and ride around in big tricycles with three wheels. And they go lots to a big building they call a wreck hall. But if it was wrecked, it's fixed now. They play games and do exercises there, but they don't do 'em very good.
>
> There's a swimming pool, and they go to it, and just stand there in the water with their hats on. I guess they

don't know how to swim. My gramma used to bake cookies 'n stuff, but I guess she forgot how. Nobody cooks. They all go to fat food places.

When you come into the park, there is a dollhouse with a man sitting in it. He watches them all day, so they can't get out without him seeing them. They wear big badges with their names on them. I guess they don't know who they are. My Gramma says Grampa worked hard all his life to be retarded. I wish they would move back home, but I guess the man in the dollhouse won't let them out.

## Achievable Genius

University of North Carolina's Harold G. McCurdy studied the development of genius for the Smithsonian Institution. He examined in detail the careers of twenty men of genius and found that they had in common several important characteristics during their early life: (1) warm, loving, and responsive attention by parents and other adults; (2) little association with children outside their families; and (3) a great deal of opportunity to explore their own interests. However, even this trio can be accentuated if the parent or teacher joins the students in a program which offers at least as much instruction time in work as in study.

## Work Skills and Brain Development

The average home and school these days poses the same problem as a one-handled wheelbarrow. Among others, La Sierra University's Linda Caviness found in her doctoral studies at Michigan's Andrews University that hands-on work experience, concurrent with study, builds unusual power in the brain. The joint effort has a synergic effect that brings higher achievement than simply adding three or four hours of work, for example, to three or four hours of study. It is like installing a second handle enables a wheelbarrow easily to carry several times the load of one with a broken handle.

We have experimented with such programs across America at all elementary and secondary levels and in colleges over the world from Central Africa and Japan to Fiji and America with astonishing records in achievement, discipline, and all-around balance and character development. Bear in mind that California's Regional Occupational Programs (ROP) were designed chiefly for delinquent kids who were devoting their days equally to work and study, and reporting the state's highest achievement records. Both parents and teachers who join youngsters in such balanced plans almost invariably find that they not only can earn a living but also are far better disciplined and mature.

## Sociability

A joint national study by Andrews and Massachusetts Universities found that 77.7 percent of homeschoolers, who are much more with their parents than peers, are in the top U.S. quartile in sociability. Balancing study, work, and service breeds entrepreneurs and social helpers who have wide social contacts at home and in communities. The Smithsonian study on genius also confirms that warm responsive parents and virtual isolation from peers, along with much creative freedom to work out their own interests are keys to developing great minds.

## Institutionalization: Big Bad Word for Bright Little Boys

The gospel of federal care, unless critically necessary, is a cruel sentence for many tots who by nature crave parental bonding. Yet most states ignore research that crosses such vested ideas. Head Start Founder Benjamin Bloom agreed, and chief psychologist Glen Nimnicht says the home, if that is possible, is altogether better than institutions. It is well established that boys are delayed a year or so in maturity at school entrance, yet states mandate their enrollment at the same ages as girls. So U.S. schools place ten to thirteen boys in special education for every girl, and there are eight emotionally impaired high school boys for every girl.

Yet boys are as bright as girls, although they are often tagged "LD—learning *disabled*" when they are more likely simply "LD—learning *delayed*." Straitjacketed into institutional life, they suffer peer ridicule, and impute parental and teacher rejection. Such boyish immaturity and adult indifference form a deadly mix. Boys of course must have family, and will find it in gangs, tobacco, alcohol and other drugs, empty sex, violence and suicide. Anyone with common sense can see why they lose what little they have of their male identity, if they have any, and thus their respect for women—obvious voids in today's society. What kind of husbands will they make? What kind of family heads? Apart from derelict homes, early schooling is an all-round cause of youth and family problems today.

## Lessons from Ancient History

Apathy and hostility to truth aren't new. In great tragic cycles, strong family societies like old China, Greece, and Rome were torn by urbane frenzies that overrode the most basic mores. Wars shifted women from home to workplace when their men left jobs to fight, leaving slaves in charge of tots and teens. We've called it "day care" since World War II. A sense of family faded; young adults banished the elderly to what China labeled "death houses." Today, worthy or not, we say "nursing homes." When Greece collapsed, family-strong Rome took over only to stumble down the same primrose path. Young couples, often hardened and thoughtless, spurned wedlock and parenthood, and jettisoned their old folks, who found out too late that the earlier you institutionalize your children, the earlier they'll institutionalize you!

With uncommon wisdom and courage, Caesar Augustus set an archetype for the ages when he wrote his Julian Laws mandating marriage and family care for both children and the aged. Harvard sociologist Carle Zimmerman and France's Frederick LePlay felt that Augustus extended the Roman Empire's viability two centuries. Augustus would have pleased Adlai Stevenson who liked to quote, "The sands of indecision bleach the bones of countless millions." Scholars fear that America is out to repeat Grecian and Roman folly. Indeed, it will collapse unless you and I place our marriage, family rights, and citizenship on the line to rebuild our society, as pioneers have done to make homeschooling the largest educational movement and performer today.

## Examples of Great Parenting

Boston College professor John Dacey and Alex Packer's four-year, mid-1990s study wraps up a synopsis for this chapter of over 750 sources and thirty-three years of homeschool pioneering. Their goal was to inspire closeness among parents and kids, hopefully motivating you to understand the Moore Formula, by practicing these methods and sharing them with other homeschools and schools. Dacey and Packer reported about families who carried out recipes similar to the Moore Formula both in homes and schools. They weighed the parenting of one hundred "highly creative children," ages five to fifteen, from fifty-six families nominated as "outstanding" from New England programs for the gifted. They found them responsible, articulate, socially adept, ethical, empathetic, confident, caring, and popular with schoolmates, hard working at home and on part-time jobs, healthy, outgoing, and achieving. In principle, God's golden rule reigned.

For a genuinely superb model that accentuates parenting, note Dacey and Packer's overall evaluation: Their methods or styles were gently and warmly authoritative, yet neither authoritarian nor permissive. They provided their children "with a clear structure of values that encourage self-discipline, commitment, and intellectual, and creative freedom." They learned and practiced the most important qualities and just naturally learned their academics brilliantly. We believe this is the best overall summary of the Moore Formula and hopefully every chapter in this book.

Note that the students in these studies were gifted. Be advised also that the so-called gifted may be described in many ways. Nearly all children are gifted in one way or another. We have proven in our application of our balanced work-study-service formula that brilliance is available for most youngsters if applied with all diligence, especially in industry and self-control.

Our goal in developing and testing the Moore Formula was that working with your children becomes your whole new life. Their imaginations are your inspiration. Trust them; exploit them as love only can. Whatever you do in the normal course of the day, do it with them and watch them flourish beyond your dreams!

Raymond S. Moore was born in Glendale, California, in September 1915. He married Dorothy Nelson in June 1938. Together they have two children and seven special kids. He attended Pacific Union College in California from 1932 to 1938, receiving his degree in English/communications. He attended the University of Southern California in 1947 where he received his M.Ed. and Ed.D. in child development, teacher education, and higher education administration.

Moore has worked on more than sixty books and monographs as author or contributor. He has held many significant positions in his life but his best accomplishment was his sixty-four-year marriage to his wife Dorothy.

# What Is Relaxed Homeschooling?

## *Mary Hood, Ph.D.*

The heart of relaxed homeschooling is more of a mind-set than a philosophy. To me the ideas involved in relaxed homeschooling can be summed up in a few basic principles:

- You're a family, not a school.
- You're a mom, not a teacher.
- You're a dad and the head of your household, not a principal.
- You don't have a classroom; you have individual relationships with your children.

Embracing these principles will not necessarily turn you into an "unschooler." Unschooling is itself a philosophy, which generally implies that parents have consciously adopted a lifestyle with few textbooks or workbooks, and no grades, tests, or labels. If I genuinely view myself as a mother, rather than a teacher, however, my own philosophy is going to take a backseat to what I know is right for each individual child.

My oldest son, Sam, was definitely unschooled at heart. He rarely opened a textbook, spent many hours outside digging in the dirt and contemplating the nature of the universe, and read incessantly without coercion. He ultimately "graduated," with no shred of evidence he had ever done anything academic, but still managed, after a few detours and a little backtracking, to obtain a degree in geology (with a minor in biology) from a public university.

However, my second son, Dan, was in almost every way the exact antithesis of my firstborn. Sam tended to be sloppy; Dan was meticulous. Sam tended to be a loner; Dan was much more social. Sam was an unschooler; Dan enjoyed using textbooks and workbooks, liked taking structured classes outside the home, and often had his own daily schedule posted on the wall of his bedroom, with no assistance from me whatsoever.

The biggest lesson I, as the mother of five children, have learned over the years is the need to treat each child completely as an individual. In the long run it doesn't really even matter what my own educational philosophy is. If I'm to do the best job I can with each of them, I must be willing to set aside my own ideas when it is necessary and trust that God will show me what to do.

My personal tendency is probably to be a "de-schooler," using a term originally coined by Ivan Illich a few decades back. I know that, whenever I pass an institutional school, I have an overwhelming urge to throw open the doors and shout, "Run! Run!" The heart of homeschooling for me is the effort to deinstitutionalize my family as much as possible. As a result, I don't really believe in "schooling" my children at all. Rather, I want to help them to develop as people. Naturally, part of that development will include academic-type knowledge. However, as a Christian, my most important goals are those involving values and the development of character. After those, I'm concerned with attitudes, habits, and the development of specific skills necessary for successful adult life. Stuffing knowledge into my kids' heads is way down on my list of what's important.

That doesn't mean that my kids wind up uneducated. They are known for possessing a wide range of knowledge and beating most of the adults whenever they play Jeopardy. However, most of the knowledge they have gained has been learned through participation in a lifestyle of learning or by engaging themselves in studies that were personally meaningful, either at home or in group settings that they selected themselves, rather than through the use of specific curriculum materials or methods that were designed for a classroom or through parent-coerced participation in outside experiences.

Other than the establishment of an interesting family life, I believe that the most important aspect of developing a relaxed homeschool is the careful delineation of goals. These goals should be carefully formulated by the parents, acting as a team. By the age of twelve or so, most children begin to develop their own goals, and these should then be woven into the fabric of education. The whole thing needs to be done together, with the children and parents acting as partners. Once these goals have been outlined, they should be the driving force behind your educational efforts, not society's ideas of "what you should be learning in your junior year."

I'm often asked, "Can a person be too relaxed?" Not only can they be, I've seen it happen all too often, when people take some of my ideas, discard the inconvenient parts, and seize the idea of sitting around in their pajamas eating popcorn all day. (This was a passing comment I made in *The Relaxed Home School*, one that I have occasionally regretted when I saw the results of being taken too literally!) When the children are young, a relaxed learning structure does not need to imply a complete lack of discipline or the absence of a work ethic. My kids are expected to accomplish great things, both academically and in other areas of their lives. I've merely found that it works a lot better when they are treated as individuals, and when I take the time prayerfully to consider the best environment for each of them in order to maximize their success at the tasks they are called to perform.

In the teen years you can certainly be too relaxed if you allow these young adults to languish in bed all day with no direction or responsibility. However, knowledge and skills can be developed in many different ways, and not every student needs to operate using a standard, one-size-fits-all curriculum. Even in the high school years, it is important to maintain family control of the learning environment and not automatically turn all decision-making over to some list of subjects found in a college catalog.

The bottom line is simply this: a relaxed family environment must be one in which the family remains dominant and is not replaced by a facsimile of a public school. After raising four children to adulthood in a relaxed homeschool atmosphere, my advice to you can be summed up as follows.

Be the best parent you can be. Ask God for guidance for each of your children as individuals. Set goals and constantly assess your progress toward those goals. Trust God's assistance, combined with your own instincts, to know what to do on a day-to-day basis for your family. If you really don't have a classroom and you really aren't a teacher or a principal, then you don't need to have everything all planned out at the start of each "school year" either. Learn to find the balance between working toward important goals and "going with the flow." Identify the assumptions about learning you have taken with you from your own public school experiences (especially grade levels, labels, tests, and pigeonholes), and throw them away. Replace them with new assumptions as you learn along with your sons and daughters. Make it a great adventure! In that manner you will learn to develop a relaxed, enjoyable environment for learning and growing together as a family at home.

Mary Hood is a veteran homeschooling mother who is the director of a homeschooling resource center in the Atlanta area. She is a sought-after workshop speaker and the author of such books as *The Relaxed Home School, The Joyful Homeschooler,* and *The Enthusiastic Homeschooler.*

Hood is also the editor of *The Relaxed Home Schooler's Newsletter.* A free sample issue can be obtained from ARCHERS, PO Box 2524, Cartersville, Georgia 30120.

# Whole-Heart Learning

*Gather me the people together, and I will make them hear my words, that they may learn to fear me all the days that they shall live upon the earth, and that they may teach their children.*

—DEUTERONOMY 4:10

❋   ❋   ❋

*I believe it would be much better for everyone if children were given their start in education at home. No one understands a child as well as his mother, and children are so different that they need individual training and study. A teacher with a roomful of pupils cannot do this. At home, too, they are in their mother's care. She can keep them from learning immoral things from other children.*

—LAURA INGALLS WILDER

The final home education method we will touch on in this manual of homeschooling styles is the whole-heart learning approach. Rather than being a method in and of itself, this approach is more a lifestyle and manner of looking at our educational options. One of the many benefits of homeschooling is tailoring each student's education much as a professional tutor would do, and the family approaching this task from the whole-heart viewpoint will set goals for the family as a whole and for each child involved in the homeschool journey.

As we will learn from Clay and Sally Clarkson, this preparation is vital to the success of the family's efforts. Rather than just choosing a curriculum for the year and saying, "We'll finish this level and then move to the next," we need to examine our overall beliefs about education, our resource options, and our end goals for the family or child. Identifying what we believe about education is paramount as these beliefs tend to color not only our teaching style but also our learning methods and those of our children. The Clarksons emphasize the heart as being the key to learning; the heart is what triggers the mind to learn and retain the information taught. What one is passionate about, one will learn. This is why Dr. Ruth Beechick reminds us of the perils of using "nonbooks." Material presented to the student that is dry and dull will not be learned; it will extinguish the fire that burns within, the fire that is fed by a love of learning.

Use of appropriate books, resources, and educational opportunities to challenge and stretch our children's mental muscles, while still keeping goals attainable, will strengthen each student's ability to proceed into life and deal with challenges and tasks to the best of his ability. Rather than making statements to us about what products we *must* use or what curricula brand we *must* have to be successful homeschoolers, our experts today will help us to realize that what we *must* do is focus on the process and avoid the pitfalls that will slow or stomp on the innate love of good books and learning that occurs in every child.

# The Dangers of Nonbooks

## Dr. Ruth Beechick

Nonbooks. What are they? A British educator wrote that all textbooks are nonbooks. First, a committee puts them together. Then more committees and pressure groups work to eliminate certain content or to add other content. This is true also of textbooks by Christian publishers who do not have to jump today's political hurdles. Even these books follow much of the world's idea of what to include in a textbook.

By contrast, real people write the real books, people with opinions and interesting things to say, whether fiction or nonfiction.

The textbook system grew as schools grew in the 1800s. It met a need for handling classrooms full of students. Now homeschoolers can suddenly be free from classroom restrictions. It takes a bit of courage and thinking outside the box. Here we will explain some specific nonbooks to omit from your homeschool.

## Reading Textbooks

Textbooks for reading have a number of disadvantages. First, they control vocabulary. This tends to slow children's progress.

Second, assignments cover only a few pages each day. Children read those pages and then perhaps fill in a few workbook blanks, thus "doing" reading for the day. By contrast, children who read real books may read many pages or even several books.

The few pages of textbook work pile up day after day and year after year. Jeanne Chall of Harvard, once the foremost reading expert, wrote that many children graduate from school thinking they have "done" reading in the same way they have "done" algebra. They have not learned to be lifetime readers.

In textbooks we lay out bits and parts of reading, hoping to include all important parts, but we do not succeed. The parts do not add up to the whole, according to Chall's research.

The best way to teach whole reading is to let children read real books. You can use some kind of beginning reading curriculum, if you wish, for the scary part of getting young children started. Once a child can read a little, let him read real books. Drop the textbook system entirely.

Do not worry that this will cause your children to miss something that is in the textbooks. Actually, the reverse is true. Children miss out if they do not have the privilege of reading real books. Once in a third-grade class, I let the children read their choice of books all year long. At the end of the year, they tested so high in reading that a primary, and even an elementary, achievement test could not assess their scores. Many of those third graders tested at junior high reading levels. And some tested at high school levels.

Do easy books improve reading ability? They certainly do. Here are two ways this works.

The first way easy reading works is to help with sight words. Even phonics zealots have to admit that children cannot easily learn many important words by phonics. Look at the word *the.* How about *was, of,* and *been?* These are sight words because it is easier to learn them by sight than to figure them out by phonics rules.

Now it happens that nine common sight words total 25 percent of the words on a page. That is true whether it is a second-grade book or a fifth-grade book, or even an adult book. Thus if children read ten pages of a simple book, they get five times as much practice on those sight words as if they read two pages in a grade-level textbook.

With the forty-one next most common words, we have a total of fifty sight words. About half of these are also phonetic. With those fifty words we have the amazing statistic that they make up 50 percent of the running words on a page, again whether it is a children's book or an adult book.[1]

Reading easy books, therefore, is a good way for children to become skilled at reading one half of the words they need to read. They also learn to spell the words because of seeing them so often.

Besides helping with sight words, easy reading helps with vocabulary growth. In a textbook lesson there may be two or three new words. At least they are presumably new for average students in a class. In easy material, by contrast, children read many more pages about many more topics. It works out that they expand their vocabulary more rapidly than if we require them to read so-called grade-level books.

When children freely choose reading material, their choices usually range from easy to difficult. For instance, they might try to read picture blurbs in a science magazine. They can skip words or ask you for help. Let them read at any and all levels that interest them.

You might have to figure out a way to start the "free" reading. It can be as simple as requiring the child to read quietly for X amount of time. My system for third graders was to have each child choose a topic, which I wrote in my grade book to make it look official. The children had to read at least three books on their topic and then tell the class in some way what they learned. The first little reports were nothing to write about, but these got better and better as the year progressed. Those children complained to me the next year that they had to read out of fourth-grade books.

One summer in my reading clinic I had a bright first grader who tested at second grade reading level. We let him read interesting books and discussed them with him. After a month he tested at fifth-grade level. The following summer he returned, still reading at fifth-grade level. A full year of classroom reading from second-grade books did nothing to improve his reading ability. A month of reading that second summer brought him up to seventh-grade level.

All children are not as bright as Johnny, but his case is a good illustration of how textbooks tend to slow the pace of children's progress.

## Literature

Some textbook publishers attempted to solve the problems mentioned above by selecting good literature to include in the books. This attempt suffered from the awkward education system of progressively forcing everything into lower grade levels. When I saw second-grade reading books asking children to identify the protagonist and antagonist and to perform other high-level analysis of the literature, I thought, *They're robbing children of their childhood!* Why can't they just enjoy the stories?

When I was a child, I loved to read more than anything. But high school literature courses spoiled the stories for me. To this day I do not know what happened in the stories that we tore apart in class.

Homeschoolers have a chance to bypass these classroom mistakes. When your children can read a little, let them read— real books—mostly simple but difficult, too.

## Phonics

What about phonics? In all my years of teaching hundreds of people to read, I never once have finished a phonics program. There comes a time with each learner when he catches on and can figure out new phonics for himself. You can help in such cases by answering children's occasional questions.

These days we overdo the systematic teaching of phonics and its rules. Young children have not yet developed their thinking abilities enough to follow through on the reasoning required to use rules. They actually do most of their phonics learning by the repetition in the courses and not by the reasoning we try to require of them.

If you are a reader, you certainly know enough phonics to teach your children how to read. Advertisements today, however, make most parents afraid of phonics. Many think they do not know it, so they spend hundreds of dollars on programs with too many bells and whistles. The high price assumes that they will be spending months, and even years, using the product. The bells and whistles imply that this glitz is needed to interest the children. If you start too early, it may take that glitz. But learning to read is exciting in itself; it does not need expensive bells and whistles.

When I was twelve years old, I taught my preschool sister how to read. I did not know enough to worry about rules. I did not think I had to go alphabetically or by any system. I just began teaching some letter sounds from the newspaper headlines each evening. It soon added up to JoAnne's reading little books. If I had read today's advertisements, I might have been afraid to enter into that fun time together.

Because of prior practice, I can teach children to read in three weeks. If you do not have prior experience, you can probably teach your child to read in about three months. The reason it does not usually work that way is due, again, to advertisements and to our society's pressure to begin too early. Research has shown that a good average time for boys to begin is about 7 1/2 years of age. Girls could begin a bit earlier. But pressures today cause people to begin at age five or earlier and then spend years and years drilling in phonics. Think of all the learning that children would achieve if they were not wasting so many hours on phonics. The ages given here are averages. Many children for various reasons should start later, while some can start earlier.

In one school district research, certain kindergarten classes spent the usual phonics time on simple science learning of baking soda, vinegar and such. The control group continued with the traditional phonics instruction. At third grade, tests showed that the "science" children read at a higher level than the others. It is easy to see the reasons for this result. The phonics children wasted a lot of time drilling on phonics, while the science children used that time to increase their vocabulary and thinking skills. They had more in their heads to bring to the reading experience.

How can you know when to begin phonics? It is quite easy. Just begin for a day or two with the lessons in your phonics program. (Use any inexpensive system; forget the bells and whistles.) If the child catches on to the lessons, then he may be ready to at least try some beginning phonics. If the lessons seem difficult and the child does not catch on quickly, then put the materials away for a few months. Do not waste time with them now. Instead, the child can learn to hand tools to Dad or to make something in the kitchen.

## Spelling Textbooks

In most spelling textbooks everybody studies the same standardized list of twenty words. Most children already know fifteen or sixteen of the words, but they must complete assignments involving all the words and take a test on all the words. Moreover, many parents soon learn that their children may pass the Friday test but still misspell one or more of the words in their writing the following week. Lists, especially standardized lists, are an ineffective way to study spelling and are a waste of time.

Where do textbook writers get the lists of twenty words? In most spelling systems the words come from children's commonly used words. So if you collect your own child's misspelled words, you have the same thing—common words—but tailored to your child's needs. When you gather spelling words this way, you must remember to use only five or fewer words for any one list. That equates with the child having to learn five words on a textbook list of twenty; if he needs to learn all the words, have a short list.

Children can collect their words into a notebook or onto cards, and you can help them study the words. Give tests only occasionally. There is no need to do this every week forever and ever. A powerful way to study a word is simply to talk about it. Why did the child spell it wrong? What can help him remember the correct spelling? Sometimes you will discover that the misspelled words cluster around one particular spelling, say *might*, *sight*, *fight*, etc. In such a case, collect those on one page of the notebook and study them as a group. You could also add an exception to the pattern: *height*.

Do not collect unusual words such as *Athabascan*. It makes sense to memorize only common words. We can look up unusual words when we need them.

Unexpected three-word spelling tests can work great if not overused. Select three words, and without letting your children see them, just give the test. Example: *girls, used to, once.* This raises all the necessary questions in children's minds. Immediately after, tell them the correct spellings, and they are likely to remember forever.

Some spelling books organize around phonics rules rather than around common words. With one of these, you and your child can browse through the book, and now and then you will find a helpful lesson. A few of the rules are highly useful, but unfortunately about 10 percent of words do not cooperate. During the teen years some vocabulary lessons on Greek and Latin prefixes, suffixes, and word roots will be valuable.

Here are three ways to individualize spelling for your children.

1. On the spot, quick teaching in the context of a child's writing
2. Individually chosen phonics or spelling-rule lessons
3. Personally collected spelling lists

## Kindergarten and Preschool Workbooks

Save your money. Never buy workbooks for young children. Oodles of research show how harmful this is. One example is that children normally do not settle their hand dominance until about age five. They should not be forced to hold a crayon in their right hand (or left) during the previous years.

One summer in my reading clinic, I had a seventh grader who read at second-grade level. After preliminary testing, I asked him if someone had forced him to be right-handed when he was young. He said, "Yes. My grandmother always made me hold a pencil in my right hand." Bill decided he would try for a while switching to his left hand. He played Ping-Pong and threw darts, and I told him to forget writing for the time being. The change turned out to be remarkably easy, and it solved his reading problem. Bill returned to school that fall reading right up to his seventh-grade level.

Other kinds of damage involve young children's eye development and other neurological development. One scholar has collected books full of information on these problems.[2]

More recent research has shown that children get burned out on workbooks if they begin in kindergarten. This shows up by third-grade level. The nonburned-out children still enjoy learning from books, but the burned-out children do not. Moreover, the children who presumably had a head start did not learn more than the others. It turned out not to be a head start at all.

So why is there such pressure upon you to get books early and start your children early? One reason, of course, is that publishers make money by selling books to you. Another reason in our society is that teachers' unions get more jobs if they can require an earlier start for children.

Actually, what you do naturally in your home is the best possible educational start for your children. You talk to the children. You take them on errands with you. You or their siblings play games with them. You read to them. Children's vocabulary and thinking skills and other development progress better in this middle-class home environment than they can in a classroom environment or in bookish pursuits. A book with ideas for parents but not fill-in blanks for children is *Language and Thinking for Young Children*.[3]

I make just one exception to the no-workbook principle, and that is when a young child wants to "do school" because older siblings are doing school. In such a case the child is just playing. Let him have short, colorful books and use them in the same way he uses toys. Do not require that he stick with the book longer than he chooses. Do not require neat work and so forth. All that can come later when it is age appropriate.

## Grammar

Grammar is a perfect example of the craziness that enters our teaching because of graded classrooms and the textbooks that followed. Once we decided to teach grammar, then we had to decide what to teach in each grade. That would have worked if we had stuck with seventh and eighth grades. But somebody had to go one better and push their grammar down to sixth grade, then fifth, and so forth.

Now we burn out the children on grammar, giving it to them before they understand it, before they have need for it, and before they can use it.

This all started back in the days when we had Latin grammar schools and students actually learned Latin and its grammar. Then came a trend toward English language schools, and by default they were called English grammar schools. Somebody had to write a book of English grammar, and the only models they had were the old books of Latin grammar. So we got books that taught about objective and subjective uses of nouns and verbs and numerous other complications that fit the Latin language but not English.

In English we only change the forms of several pronouns to indicate whether they are objects or subjects. So we do not need to teach the entire Latin system of subjective and objective "cases" as they are called. The sensible system would be to teach students how to use the few pronouns. Actually, English teachers became more sensible in the 1960s and simplified the textbooks to make them fit the English language instead of Latin. Naturally, there was a backlash. How dare we water down the curriculum?

Somehow we cannot manage to teach even the pronouns. One of the most common errors that preachers and others make in speech is to say, "He called Bob and I." My guess is that this comes from overteaching formal grammar. People learn to say *I* at the end of a sentence because they learn to say, "Bob is older than I," meaning, "Bob is older than I am." They also learn not to say, "me and Bob," so it must be "Bob and I."

The simple way to teach that usage is to try it without the name Bob. We all would say, "He called *me*." Thus we should say, "He called Bob and *me*." That does not take any grammar explanation; it only takes a native ear for English. The grammar explanation includes the following: *called* is a transitive verb, which requires a direct object. *Me* is that direct object. Thus we must use the objective form of the pronoun. How much easier to use the native ear system!

That native ear for English will take care of practically all grammar needs while children learn to speak and write well. Once they speak and write well, say about seventh or eighth grade, then they can understand what grammar books are saying. If they were not burned out on grammar in the meantime, they might actually enjoy the study.

So forget about buying grammar books grade by grade. Instead, buy one reference book to use through all the years. A good choice for the elementary school years is *Learning Grammar through Writing*.[4] This is for grades three through eight and is available from several homeschool suppliers. Children can gradually learn how to look up information in such a book, and it can earn a place as a reference book alongside the dictionary. You and the children will appreciate such a book more than the used workbooks that become useless in afterlife for looking up information. In the teen years, you might add a good college English handbook. One easy-to-use book is *Harbrace College Handbook*.[5] If you live near a college bookstore, you will find several good reference books from which to choose. You could add interesting books on writing style to your collection, such as *The Elements of Style.*[6]

When I say to delay grammar teaching, I refer to the narrow meaning of grammar: the study of parts of speech and parts of sentences. Children need writing mechanics, things like punctuation and capitalization. And they need occasional usage correction. (Don't say *ain't.*) These can mix with grammar, but usually the ear approach will teach whatever your children need.

## Writing

Writing is a mixed bag when it comes to buying curriculum. The first lesson for most children is to trace or copy their own names from a model you make. They soon graduate to sentences: *God is love.* Use copying and dictation a lot,[7] but also let the children write their own stories when they want to.

After the sentence level, the main thing about writing is to have something to say. In classes, I used to handle this by assigning a topic like, "What I did during vacation." That is a boring topic and too often results in list writing: "I went swimming, took a trip to New York, played baseball, and played around."

Later I solved the problem by handing it over to the children. It is amazing that the most successful learning projects I remember are those that took the least preparation on my part. In this case I told the class that they had to hand in some writing every day. They quickly worked out how to do it. For instance, if a dog did something funny, they would latch on to that as a topic and write it the next day in school. The best I could do was to show interest and react to their stories.

Among homeschool curriculums are several good courses teaching how to write. My general comment on these is that no one course can do it all. Writing is too broad and has too many approaches. Somebody tells children to organize before they write. Somebody else says to start with a first draft and then go through the process of rewriting. Somebody else tells them how to embed phrases to make more complex sentences. And the next person tells them to simplify their sentences.

So my best suggestion about curriculum is to use a book when you want to and find help in it. But set aside the book whenever you have real-life writing to do, such as a missionary day when the whole family sits down to write letters to missionaries.

At higher levels some curriculums do a good job of teaching how to write an essay or a research report or other forms. Professional writers constantly work to improve. Your family can always learn something new also.

## Arithmetic

Even in arithmetic, you gain by delaying textbooks. On any list of what your first grader should learn, you likely would see that he already knows most of the items.

For instance, one listed item is that children should learn to add two groups up to sums of six. If three plates are on the table and the child sets one or two more, how many plates are on the table? If two people are in the front seat of the car and two more climb in the back, how many is that altogether?

This kind of arithmetic uses concrete thinking. Children see real objects. They can touch and count them. This way they build a strong foundation of arithmetic understanding.

Time and repeated experiences at the concrete stage of learning move children into the next stage where they use mental images. They can visualize plates in their heads and do not need to see or touch actual objects.

Only after the concrete stage and the mental image stage are children ready for the abstract stage. They can then think of a group of three. It does not have to be plates or people or anything with a name. Just add to the group of three. The digit 3 can stand for the group.

The trouble with arithmetic workbooks is that they begin with this abstract stage. Instead of working with plates, they work with $3 + 2 = 5$. The groups are abstract. The digits are abstract. And the plus and equal signs are abstract.

This leads to a lot of time memorizing the "facts" of addition, subtraction, and later of multiplication. If you move more slowly through the concrete stages, your children build understanding, and they will not have to memorize and drill and practice and memorize some more. They will understand what is going on in the problems.

Many books try to begin concretely by using pictures, but that is difficult to do. Abstractions become mixed in, even in the best of books.

So to get this strong start in arithmetic, skip workbooks for kindergarten and earlier. Then skip workbooks for first grade. If you grow comfortable with this system, skip workbooks for second grade also. For your own peace of mind, you could use the checklist below. Or you could look at a workbook one page at a time and do the problems with real objects. Omit the pencil and paper part. Just let the child tell you how many are in two groups of blocks or marbles or whatever real objects you have available.

At the time of this writing, homeschoolers have been successful in most states in seeing that achievement test requirements begin at third grade. So the pencil and paper abstract notations can wait until third grade also. Children will learn them more rapidly then. Furthermore, they will learn with understanding and not just through drills and memory work.

Another testing option in most places is the portfolio. In these cases a teacher talks with children to determine whether they are making progress. Of course they always are; you cannot stop young children from learning. In the portfolio, keep a list of the child's arithmetic abilities. For instance, one item can say, "Adds two groups up to sums of six." Or to sums of ten. The child can demonstrate with blocks.

If after all these arguments you still want to begin early with books, I suggest using *Making Math Meaningful*.[8] These books do the best job of teaching for meaning and understanding rather than just memory and computation procedures. They continue the meaning approach on through the higher levels of math.

## Arithmetic Checklist[9]

PRESCHOOL TO GRADE THREE

- Counts to 10___, to 100___, to 200___. More than just chanting, the child must be able to count out 15 sheets of paper, etc.
- Uses and understands ordinal numbers up to 10th___. Examples: We are *3rd* in line; it's the *5th* house on the left. On calendars may go up to 30th___.
- Recognizes groups such as dots on dominoes or dice: up to 5___, to 10___.
- Adds two groups up to sums of 6___, to 10___, to 12___.
- "Takes away" a group from 6 and tells what is left___, from 10___, from 12___. (Do not do the other kind of subtraction yet—the kind that compares two items and asks how much larger or smaller one is.)
- Counts by twos to 10___, or higher___. Use pairs to practice this: ___eggs in a carton, ___socks in pairs.
- Counts by fives and tens to 30___, to 100___. Use an abacus, piles of checkers, nickels and dimes.

- Experiences the use of nickels___, dimes___, quarters___, ruler (inches only)___, feet (no fractions)___, time in hours___, half hours___, whole measuring cups and spoons___.
- Understands a fractional part of apple, candy bar, etc.: 1/2___, 1/4___, 1/3___ (only numerators of 1).
- Uses words of quantity, size, and shape: tall, taller, tallest___, large, larger, largest___, less, more___, top, bottom___, circle___, square___, hour___, minute___, other___. *Advanced concepts:* add___, plus___, equals___, subtract___, minus___, left, right___, dozen___, quart___, pint___, pounds___, others___.
- Solves real-life problems___. Examples: What coins do we need to buy this stamp? Do we have all the books to return to the library?

ADVANCED

(Use after most of the above are checked.)

- Reads digits from 1 to 10___, to 30___, to 100___, writes digits to 10___, to 30___, to 100___.
- Writes addition and subtraction problems in horizontal sentence form___, and vertical form___. Examples:

$$4 + 2 = 6 \qquad \begin{array}{r} 4 \\ +\,2 \\ \hline 6 \end{array}$$

- Understands two times a group___, three times___. Can divide a larger group into twos___, into threes___, fives___, tens___. (Use real objects only, not written problems.)

## Science and Social Studies

In this section I lump together all the content subjects. So far we have looked at the skill subjects and considered that children learn to read by reading, to write by writing, and so forth.

Now with content subjects we can take a different attitude toward books. Books are more helpful in teaching content than in teaching skills. Today we have a rich choice of books.

From your own schooling, you probably already are biased against textbooks. Most of us have come through school feeling that history is a dull subject. Our textbooks were dull because they skimmed too quickly over too many topics. These are prime examples of nonbooks. Some teachers enriched the textbook study with real books or videos, and many homeschoolers now do the same. Better yet, many begin with real books and refer to a text only for ideas about topics to teach or for a quick summary of a topic.

There is absolutely no reason for a fifth grader to study American colonial history or a sixth grader to study South America, and so on. Schools lay out what they call scope and sequence for the simple purpose of trying to cover all important topics somewhere in the curriculum. Even so, they cannot cover all important topics. And if it is dull, children do not learn a lot of it anyway.

You lose nothing by switching topics around for your family's convenience. And you lose nothing by emphasizing topics that are important to you. Be cautious of following the outlines in modern texts. They have switched to teaching globalism rather than patriotism to one's own country. And they have switched to other politically correct views, such as that Islam's god is similar to Christianity's God. Sadly, many Christian schoolbooks include some of these views too. Worldview testing shows that children's views of God and country went steeply downhill during the 1990s, in Christian schools as well as public schools.

Homeschooling is our best stronghold for teaching biblical worldviews, and these content subjects are where you do it. For science, use materials from the creationist writers and organizations. With this background your children will understand even evolution better than children who learn from only the evolutionary view. In history, government, and other social subjects, use only books by Christian writers. There are enough good ones that there is no point in diluting your teaching by using anything else.[10]

You and your family are our nation's best hope for the future. Make the most of these years with your children.

## Endnotes

1. The fifty words are listed in Ruth Beechick, *The Three R's*, from www.homeschoolingbooks.com (810-714-4280).

2. Raymond S. Moore, et. al., *Better Late than Early: A New Approach to Your Child's Education* (New York, NY: E. P. Dutton, 1989) and *School Can Wait* (Provo, UT: Brigham Young University, 1989).

3. Ruth Beechick and Jeannie Nelson, *Language and Thinking for Young Children*, Homeschooling Books. See note 1.

4. Sandra Bell, *Learning Grammar through Writing* (Cambridge, MA: Educators Publishing Service, 1989).

5. John C. Hodges, et. al., *Harbrace College Handbook*, 13th ed. (Orlando, FL: Harcourt Brace Jovanovich, 1998).

6. William Strunk and E. B. White, *The Elements of Style* (New York, NY: Macmillan, 2000).

7. Detailed instructions for this are given in Beechick, *The Three R's* and *You Can Teach Your Child Successfully.*

8. David Quine, *Making Math Meaningful*, www.cornerstonecurriculum.com (972-235-5149).

9. Compiled from Beechick, *The Three R's.*

10. Cornerstone Curriculum is a good source of worldview books for teens by David Quine. See note 8.

\* \* \*

Dr. Ruth Beechick has taught children of all ages and taught as education professor at a Christian college. She also spent a number of years developing and writing curriculum. When the homeschool movement came along, she could see that home-schoolers needed their own family approach to teaching and not a classroom approach. Her writings explaining this better way have influenced homeschoolers themselves and the curriculum publishers among them. She believes that homeschooling is the strongest education today, and she sees homeschoolers as a great hope for the future of our society.

# The Power of Books
# and Reading

*Sally Clarkson*

Our Sunday afternoon teatimes seem naturally to stimulate conversations that are as strong and satisfying as the hot English tea, as tasty and filling as the blueberry scones smothered in clotted cream and boysenberry jam, and sometimes as heated as the fire on the grate. This Sunday, though, it was more of a cozy, warm fire as we all reveled in a feast of thoughts and opinions born of books and reading. Sarah, twenty, shared insights from a new physics book that is profoundly expanding her understanding of God's universe. Joel, seventeen, excitedly reported on a fascinating article about the history of the Irish and their need for Bible teaching. Nathan, fifteen, while rolling on the floor with our dog Kelsey, offered a rousing narration of an adventurous English novel, capped with the admonition, "You need to read it out loud to Joy; she would love it!" Joy, nine, who was designing small throw pillows for each of us as spring gifts, proudly announced, "I read three books this weekend— one about trees, a biography about Teddy Roosevelt, and a fun picture book." We even managed to do some reading aloud from James Herriot before calling it an afternoon teatime.

That Sunday afternoon is a snapshot of what goes on throughout the week in our home. Since opinions and convictions are never in short supply, discussions and conversations can break out at any time. They are generally energetic and articulate, sometimes loud, and fraught with passion, humor, and strong opinion. Most of all they are all highly enjoyable. I sat on the couch next to Clay, marveling at the very interesting, intelligent, passionate, pure-hearted, and loving young adults that our children have become. After so many years of investing in their lives, it is exciting for me to see the fruit of that labor bursting out of my children.

From the beginning of my parenting and homeschooling journey, I always hoped and prayed that my children would grow up to become more than just "educated" by the world's standards. I longed to raise godly young adults who loved learning and possessed an inner drive to keep learning all their lives. I wanted to raise lifelong seekers of wisdom, knowledge, discernment, and understanding. I suppose that desire really started when I moved to Europe as a young single missionary. It was so obvious that young people there knew much more history, literature, music, and art than the average American-educated child. We had been taught well how to fill in the blanks on tests yet not necessarily as well about how to read widely, think critically, synthesize research, explain our views, or defend a cohesive and coherent worldview.

Even before I began having children, I knew that I wanted them to have a different kind of education. As a new young mother, with a heart full of biblical ideals and convictions from my years in ministry and missions, I sensed God had a new direction for my children than what I had known growing up. In my quest to discover it, I was driven to read every book and article

I could find. Homeschooling was still in its infancy so I read whatever books I could find about the movement. Mostly, though, I studied the Scriptures and read from a wide variety of sources to learn as much as I could about childhood learning, how to stimulate creativity and intelligence, and how to instill a love for learning in my children.

In all of my reading and research, one factor stood out and was almost universally affirmed—the power of books, reading, and reading aloud. I became overwhelmingly convinced that books would be a key component of their education. I would read often and regularly from great books of all kinds, discuss the great ideas and thoughts in them, and engage my children's hearts and minds in the adventure of learning from real books. It seemed clear to me that because God designed us from eternity past to be people of his book (the Bible), that we are designed as well to learn from all books. The written Word is God's chosen method for teaching his children. Books would be my curriculum for teaching my children.

That decision would set me swimming against the tide. As an education major in college, I had been equipped to use standard, classroom-tested, age-graded curriculum and textbooks. "Real books" were nice, but in that environment they were only supplemental. But now that I was a mother, I instinctively realized that I wanted much more for my children than what I had been trained to give in a school setting. I wanted them to have a "living education" full of great books, real life, and real relationships. It would be harder, perhaps, and require more involvement in my children's lives, but I took the step of faith and embarked on a living and learning adventure with my children that is still going on. Not only am I pleased with what it has done for my children, but I love how it has shaped our family experience. We are living to learn, learning to live, loving each other, and loving books . . . all together!

You can also read Clay's article on "WholeHearted Home Education" to see how we fleshed out the power of reading in our own discipleship-based and home-centered approach to home education. We call our approach WholeHearted Learning, but we have noticed many parents we talk with describe themselves as "whole bookers." If you ever hear someone talk about a whole book approach to home education, they are simply describing a book-centered approach to learning at home that emphasizes reading and discussing literature and "living" books. It is more than that, of course (see our WholeHearted Learning Model), but it affirms the absolute necessity of real books and reading in learning. We, too, are whole-bookers.

Since our cultural default for education is workbooks and textbooks, though, many young mothers will ask me, "Why do you think books are so important? Aren't you afraid there will be holes in your children's education?" Each time I'm asked that, I find myself revisiting the issue and reflecting on why I have chosen this path. I always come away with an even deeper conviction that books and reading are the keys to unlocking real learning. As to the "holes," of course there will be some— no educational model is without holes! Unlike curricular models, though, which sometimes leave gaping holes from a book-deficient approach, a book-rich approach that emphasizes self-learning from whole books will be a self-mending model— learning never stops, as it does at the end of a workbook, but continues for a lifetime. There are many more reasons books are the keys to learning than I have space to discuss here (many are in our book *Educating the WholeHearted Child*), but let me share a few of the convictions that keep me passionate about books and reading.

## Books Are Whole Food for a Child's Spirit, Heart, and Mind

Great literature is the natural food for a child's mind. It is complete (a whole book, not just snippets of information condensed into a few paragraphs), satisfying (using real words and ideas with complete sentences and thoughts), and interesting (a complete, complex, well-told story or well-explained idea). Through great literature, a child is exposed to the best writers and thinkers throughout history.

A person who writes a whole book does so because he has a passion about a subject, and the personal experience to add authenticity and validity to knowledge. A child's mind has an enormous capacity and hunger for learning that can be satisfied by life-changing ideas and heartfelt stories found in great books. The wider the exposure to great thinkers and their thoughts, the greater the impact on a child's developing mind. As a person created in God's image, a child has an innate desire for great thoughts and ideas that stretch his capacity to think and that will develop his mental muscles.

## Books That Engage the Heart Bring Life to the Reader

Books can be either lifeless or living, depending upon whether they engage only the mind, or the heart, too. Remember, the Word of God is "*living* and active . . . able to judge the thoughts and intentions of the *heart*" (Heb. 4:12 NASB, emphasis added). A textbook is usually written in an impersonal way with the primary purpose of surveying and summarizing selected facts. In most cases textbooks are lifeless books; they engage only the mind with facts and data, reducing the process of learning about a subject to memorizing a collection of loosely connected details.

Because nothing connects those facts to the heart, they are quickly forgotten. Can you think of anything you know now because of a textbook or of a textbook that changed your heart? I can't.

A living book, in contrast, engages both heart and mind. It is usually written by a single author who has a passion to share about his subject rather than designed by a textbook committee. A motivated author, who knows how to use language powerfully and effectively, can include connections to real life and real experiences, sharing his or her heart impressions and personal knowledge about the subject. Because the heart of the author is engaged in the writing, the heart of the reader is drawn into the subject and windows of understanding are opened. Long after the facts and pieces of information in a textbook are read and forgotten, the insights, ideas, word pictures, stories, and relationships from a living book will be locked into a child's memory. Living books live on in children's minds and have the power to change their hearts.

## Books Provide an Endless Source of Learning That Will Last a Lifetime

My desire, as a home educator, is to raise readers of living books. I want my children to become self-learners, possessing a heartfelt desire and even a passion to always want to read and learn. That means my real goal in education, in the words of poet William Butler Yeats, "is not the filling of a bucket but the lighting of a fire." My goal is not to be content because my children fill up countless workbooks with book work but to be content only when I know I am filling up hearts with captivating, interesting, and satisfying learning that comes from reading real, living books. God has put within their hearts a burning desire for purpose and greatness, and great books are the kindling for building it into a fire in their young hearts. Textbooks full of dry facts will smother that flame; real books, shared in the fellowship of family reading together, will feed it and keep it burning strong. The flame burns strong in our family because we have fed it with many whole books that have captivated all of us in the adventure and interest of real-life drama, have drawn us into the world of great ideas and movements, and have fed the imagination of our own dreams.

## Books Are Treasure Troves of Godly, Moral, and True Thoughts and Examples

When I picture my children's spirits, hearts, and minds, I see a large chest that I am filling with lasting treasures and memories. My desire is to give them a treasure chest full of resources from which they can draw the rest of their lives. Of course, the richest resources are the love of family and the biblical truths and godly character I continually put there. Next to those, though, are the treasures that come from reading books. By reading great books, I am filling their treasure chests with hero tales of men and women who have accomplished great feats throughout history. In a day when role models are hard to come by, living books can step into the gap with stories about men and women who exhibit godliness, morality, boldness, and leadership—heroes who call us by their lives to follow their examples.

I am also filling their chests with deep thoughts about God, life, people, and history. From the repository of ideas in the great books that I select for them, my children will find rich resources that will begin to shape their own messages, guide their decisions, inform their biblical worldview, and deepen their understanding of moral goodness. And, in a day when language and beauty are pushed aside by contemporary culture, I can enrich their lives by filling their chests with exposure to beautiful and thoughtful poetry, outstanding literature, biblically sound apologetics, and skillfully expounded ideas. Rather than being shaped by an illiterate and image-driven culture, I will call on the power of books and reading to pattern their own intellects after great thinkers and leaders.

## Books Build Vocabulary, Strengthen Grammar, Aid Spelling, and Shape Writing

Children who are read to, and who develop the habit of reading, often score higher on aptitude and scholastic tests. The repeated exposure to excellent writing, broad vocabulary, and skillful mechanics establishes patterns, or highways of thinking, in a child's brain. Young children do not develop vocabulary by memorizing lists of discreet words; they will develop vocabulary best by hearing and using words in the context of real language. They form word meanings in their minds naturally in the same way that they learn a language from their parents when they are babies.

Children who read and are read to are much more likely to be articulate and able to communicate ideas both verbally and in writing. Their language skills are strongly influenced by hearing and reading classic books and literature. Excellence is catching! In contrast, age-graded textbooks dumb down vocabulary and simplify abstract thoughts to the lowest levels of ability expected in a classroom of that child's age. Mediocrity and conformity are the cultural norms in the classroom, but research shows that children are able to understand concepts and words in a much more mature form than they are able to articulate. That is why it is important to give them the best in living books, knowing that that their mental muscles will stretch to a higher degree than is expected of them in an age-graded environment. Rather than relying on tedious language arts workbooks with lessons divorced from life, real books provide models and "lessons" I can use to bring language arts to life for my children.

## Books Provide Models for How to Use Words Powerfully and Skillfully

The power of language is the ability to use words to move people—to cause another person to learn, to change, to act, to resist, to believe or to follow. It is true of children as well. Whatever a child becomes is because of the power of the language and the words that are influencing and forming the ideas of his or her life. Whatever impact your children will have for God in their generation will be to a great extent shaped by the truths and ideas you plant in their hearts and minds and the language skills you give them to communicate clearly. Whether they become great thinkers, great speakers, or great writers, their thoughts about God, his Word, and his purposes will be only as deep as the language they study and use that will give form and voice to their thoughts.

In a culture in which the vocabulary and language skills of children and youth decline a little more with each passing year, we can raise articulate, thoughtful children who will stand apart as they move into adulthood and leadership. The "secret" for seeing that happen is as old as the Bible; it is an education at home centered on reading and books. One study found that the common factor in the childhood of those who are considered geniuses is exposure and access to many books. A well-stocked library is a first step toward raising a child who will stand apart and who will know how to use words to change lives and perhaps change the world.

## Books Provide a Means for Family Fellowship and Personal Growth

One of the most satisfying benefits of reading whole books is that our whole family has become closer and more unified. When we read a great book aloud together, we all share in the adventure, excitement, and emotional experiences of the author through his life or through his characters' lives. It creates a common experience in our relationship with one another. I don't have to pick only immature books for my little ones and a different set of books for my older children. When we read together, we grow together and share the same memories and ideas in our minds. These ideas then flow naturally into the daily discussions that we have at the dinner table or in the car or on vacations, and no one is left on the outside of the discussions. Everyone is involved. As I have learned right along with my children, I have been amazed at how we have all become soul mates from our many times of reading or listening to books on tape together. People have been educated in this way for generations, but our culture has just forgotten the incredible power of learning through books.

There are so many more reasons to read whole books to your children, but it would take a whole book to tell them! The more you explore the rich treasures of books and literature with your children in a whole book approach, the more you will wonder how you could ever consider another way. It takes a step of faith to let go of the security of textbooks and workbooks, but you will never regret leaving that path to take the journey of learning through real books and real life. But regardless of what path of educational philosophy you follow, you can always leave room for reading real books together. When you see how whole books ignite your child's love for learning right in your own living room, it won't be long before your library begins to grow . . . right along with your whole family.

❋  ❋  ❋

Sally Clarkson is the mother of four wholehearted children, a popular conference speaker, and the author of numerous books and articles on motherhood, including *The Mission of Motherhood, The Ministry of Motherhood, Seasons of a Mother's Heart,* and *Educating the WholeHearted Child* (with Clay).

Sally has been involved in ministry since college and in her marriage since 1981. In 1994, she and Clay founded Whole Heart Ministries to encourage and equip Christian parents. Since 1998, she has ministered to thousands of mothers through her WholeHearted Mother Conferences.

The Clarksons live in Monument, Colorado and have home-schooled all of their children from the beginning.

# Wholehearted Home
# Education

### *Clay Clarkson*

H ow long have you been homeschooling?" Most parents, to answer that typical icebreaker question, have no problem pinpointing the year they began their journey. Not so for us. Even though we are many years down the road now, with two graduates under our homeschooling belt and two more in process, I still hesitate to set a date when it all began.

The easy answer is 1988, when we joined our first home-school support group for our firstborn child, Sarah. But then, I'm sure we were homeschoolers in 1982, when I read a magazine article about Christian homeschooling while at Denver Seminary and told Sally we should consider it. Sally started reading Dr. Raymond Moore's books and soon taught a church class on homeschooling before her first pregnancy. But then, she did that because in 1975, six years before we would marry and start a family, we both went on staff with Campus Crusade for Christ after college. Strong convictions about discipleship, biblical lifestyle, and personal ministry were burned into our hearts that would set the course for our life's journey. Even though we didn't know it at the time, I believe that is when we really started homeschooling. That is when we caught a vision for the Christ-centered life.

Long before our first child reached school age, we had already sensed the course of our lives as parents. We had already rejected the cultural notion that homeschooling was simply an "alternative education." It was never an issue for us of tallying up the pros and cons on a yellow legal pad to see which would win—public, private, or home. From the beginning we knew homeschooling was a biblical lifestyle, not just an alternative education. If the Christ-centered life applied to all parts of our lives, then homeschooling was the natural and obvious expression of it in our family life. Our children were our most important disciples, a personal ministry given to us by God, and it was clear to us from Scripture that the divinely designed institution where that would happen was home and family.

We read many books, listened to other homeschooling families, searched the Scriptures, discussed and prayed as we evaluated various models of homeschooling. What concerned us most was that so many were overly "academic" models that we felt were based on a faulty premise, that homeschooling "success" should be measured by knowledge and intellect. That certainly did not seem to reflect any biblical standard we could find, and it seemed those models often generated an artificial lifestyle that was less like home and more like school. We believed that homeschooling, if it truly was a movement of God, would be radically different from the world's models of family and education. There should be no artificial distinction between living and learning, as though those were two separate spheres of experience. We wanted a holistic and wholehearted model of family life that brought everything together literally under one roof. When we couldn't find it, we set about designing our own model.

## Distinctives of WholeHearted Learning

We began by identifying our assumptions about learning. These are just a few of them. First, we believed that the heart is the key to all learning. Solomon clearly has the heart in view when he says, "The fear of the LORD is the beginning of knowledge: but fools despise wisdom and instruction" (Prov. 1:7). Fifteen times in the first nine chapters of Proverbs, when addressing his sons directly, he emphasizes the preeminence of the heart in the process of gaining wisdom and understanding. If, in God's design, the heart directs what the mind learns, we wanted to be sure we would give our children whole and healthy hearts for God.

Second, we believed that Scripture clearly shows that the natural place for a child and a young adult to learn is home and family. There is simply no biblical model for the abdication of parental responsibility to other institutions that has become the norm in our culture. God intended parents to be the authorities, instructors, guidance counselors, protectors, and principals in their children's lives. God did not somehow forget to include school in his divine design; it simply wasn't needed. He had already designed the family and home. We wanted to be sure our children grew up in a wholehearted Christian home.

Third, we believed children are designed by God to learn first and best through real life and real relationships (family, friends, church, and community). The hunger and thirst for knowledge is inherent in a child and needs to be released and directed, not controlled and conformed. Too much formalism in learning turns what God intended to be a natural process into a mental chore robbed of all joy. We wanted our children to love learning and to become self-learners, not just be good test-takers. We wanted to raise wholehearted learners.

Fourth, we believed children, and all people for that matter, are wired by God to learn from books. Because we are designed to learn about God and life from his book, the Bible, we are by default designed to learn from all books. Not only would we want to fill our children's lives with books, but they would be good books, real books that would feed their hunger for knowledge with ideas and insights, not textbooks filled with fragmented bits of information. We call them "whole books" and "living books" because they are nutritious and satisfying.

When we observed how our children learned, we saw that they naturally loved reading and being read to, talking about their own insights and ideas, learning through real life, and having lots of time to explore and learn on their own. The more we studied Scripture and observed our children, the more confident we became that this was how God designed children to live and learn. It was obvious, though, that we were headed in a new direction, away from anything that we had ever known before.

## Building Mental Muscles

It's always hard to switch paradigms, and when all we've known as a culture is the classroom model, switching to a relational, home-centered model of learning can test our confidence. The most common concern is usually whether average parents can do "enough" to really educate their child—"How will I know if my children know everything they need to know?" That concern does not originate from Scripture but rather from a culture obsessed with measuring learning. But the truest measure of learning is not what a child knows at any one time relative to what other children know; it is whether that child is growing stronger in all of the most important learning skills. We like to call them "mental muscles."

Just as children have varying physical abilities, they also have varying mental abilities. Some children will be naturally stronger physically than others, but we do not insist on measuring and comparing all children's arm muscles or their ability to lift things. Neither should we compare and judge all children on the basis of one or two mental muscles. The goal should be to exercise all of a child's mental muscles so they will enter adulthood with a strong mind, with the desire (will) and the ability (skill) to learn whatever is necessary, whatever the situation. Performing well in comparison to other children in an artificial classroom setting is no indication that a child will perform well in real life in comparison to other adults.

The goal of education is not to raise a child who does well on the tests of secular educators but to raise a child who does well on the tests of real life. When they need to research an issue, they will have the discipline and ability to find and analyze relevant information. When they need to present an argument, they will know how to use language persuasively. When mediating a problem at church, they will know how to apply wisdom and find a creative solution. Knowledge is the natural fruit of growing stronger mental muscles, not the other way around.

And what are the mental muscles? Certainly there are more than these, but we have found seven that we think are critical to mental strength:

> Habits—the ability instinctively to act upon common duties or tasks without being told
>
> Appetites—the ability to discern and desire what is excellent and worthy
>
> Language—the ability clearly to articulate and communicate ideas and beliefs
>
> Creativity—the ability to reflect the image and glory of God in all that one does

Curiosity—the ability to question, to seek out knowledge, and to keep learning

Reason—the ability to think clearly and logically about ideas, decisions, and life

Wisdom—the ability to apply spiritual insight and discernment in any situation

## The WholeHearted Learning Model

The question remaining then, of course, is what kind of home education model would best allow for the expression of these convictions and observations about living and learning at home, and the strengthening of mental muscles. Before I describe what emerged from our own search, let me remind you that we are not educational theoreticians creating some arcane academic model but rather simply observers of human nature (our children's) and chroniclers of common sense. The model we developed consists of five areas of focused studies. To use the metaphor of a house, the first area is the foundation, the middle three are the interior structures, and the final area is the roof.

**1. Discipleship Studies**—We start with the study of God's Word to gain wisdom. Our goal is "to shape our children's hearts to love God and to study and know his Word." This is the "beginning of knowledge" that Solomon refers to (Prov. 1:7). It encompasses devotions, Bible stories, topical Bible studies, Bible knowledge, and more. Without this "foundation," the house we build would not stand long (Matt. 7:24–27).

**2. Disciplined Studies**—Next we study the basics, such as math and language arts, that require a more disciplined approach. Our goal is "to develop our children's foundational learning skills and competencies." Some studies can benefit from more formal methods and materials, but we keep it short and look for more natural methods, too. This area is like the structural frame of the house that defines and shapes it.

**3. Discussion Studies**—Then we spend the bulk of our studies in the humanities, reading and reading aloud literature and history, and studying the fine arts. Our goal is "to feed our children's minds on the best in living books and the fine arts." This is the heart of our model, where most of the time is spent. Reading aloud is an important part of the learning process, so we are always reading through a book. This is area like the load-bearing walls that keep the house from falling in on itself.

**4. Discovery Studies**—After that we can direct our children into areas such as nature, science, the creative arts, and all other interests. Our goal is to stimulate in our children a love for learning by creating opportunities for curiosity, creativity, and discovery. We have discovery corners throughout our house to encourage more self-directed, but still parent-guided, studies. This area is like the ceilings in the home that help define and shape the interior space.

**5. Discretionary Studies**—Finally, we turn to the "study of living," focusing on natural gifts and interests, community involvement, lessons, and life skills. Our goal is to direct our children in developing a range of skills and abilities according to their drives and gifts. This is where we look at each child and help all of them discover how God has specially gifted them, develop in their own areas of ability, and determine how to use that skill for God's glory. This final area is the roof of the house that completes it.

## More Than Schooling

It was never our goal to mimic classroom schooling simply because it was the only thing we knew but rather to discover the divinely designed dynamic of the home for living and learning with our children. We believe that any home can and should be a warm, vibrant place where children love to learn as freely and as naturally as they love to play. If, in fact, education is the natural outgrowth of the discipleship relationship between parents and children, then it should be the natural activity of every Christian home. That is what this "wholehearted learning" model tries to capture.

There is great freedom in knowing that what you are doing is going along with a pattern that is already built into the fabric and rhythm of your lives by God. He has designed your children to learn; he has designed your home to be a learning environment; and he has designed you to be a learning guide. Joy and freedom naturally follow when we cooperate with God's design. That is why our goal has never been to become great homeschoolers but rather to be the most biblical, effective, fruitful Christian "home builders" we could be.

In our home, we've identified three priorities of Christian home building. Each of these three priorities builds upon the one before it and supports the one following it. If you feel God is putting home education on your heart, the place to start is not with choosing a homeschooling curriculum or approach. If you want a biblical plan for home education, start with a vision for a truly Christian home. Here are the priorities we've identified for our home:

### HOME NURTURE: SHEPHERDING YOUR CHILD'S SPIRIT TO LONG FOR GOD

Home nurture is the process of creating a Christ-centered atmosphere and environment in your home. You begin to integrate Christ and Scripture into every area of your family life—family devotionals, spiritual traditions, close relationships, or even how you decorate your home. It includes developing your child's character, as well as being sure your own spiritual well is filled up. In a sense home nurture is enriching the spiritual air your children will breathe in your home. You are shepherding your child's heart, cultivating a longing for God and openness to his truth, a necessary part of a truly Christian education.

## HOME DISCIPLESHIP: SHAPING YOUR CHILD'S HEART TO LIVE FOR GOD

Home discipleship is the intentional process of leading your child to follow and serve Christ as Lord. It is one thing to know the language and lifestyle of Christianity, but it is quite another to know Christ. Home discipleship is how you as a parent not only instruct your children about Christ but also model the life of Christ for them and lead them into a relationship and daily walk with him. You do that by studying Scripture together, reading and discussing inspiring and challenging Christian books, and getting involved in church and community ministry as a family. Remember, a *disciple* of Christ is not a technical term; it means, literally, a "learner."

## HOME EDUCATION: STRENGTHENING YOUR CHILD'S MIND TO LEARN FOR GOD

Home education, then, is simply the natural outgrowth of home nurture and home discipleship. Your goal, though, is not just an educated child, good SATs, and college, or even a career and a good salary. Those may be fruits of your efforts, but your overriding goal is to raise spiritually mature children who are ready to love and follow Christ with all their heart, soul, mind, and strength. Your goal in home education is to raise a well-rounded, spiritually grounded, truth-founded Christian whose goal in life is to make a difference for the kingdom of God, whatever life path he or she chooses. God has chosen you to give your children that kind of education.

Unfortunately, it is at this third priority that many families, wanting to do the right thing, choose the wrong way. Rather than trusting that God has designed the home to be a complete living and learning environment, they try to retrofit the institutional classroom model into it. But a home is not a school! God designed the home, man designed the school—they were never meant to fit together. Only in the home, just as God designed it, can you shepherd your children's spirits to long for him, shape their hearts to live for him, and strengthen their minds to learn for him—all at the same time, all the time! God did not leave anything out of the home your children would need.

If you have a biblical mandate as a Christian parent to influence your child for God (Deut. 6:1–9; Eph. 6:1–4), then it makes no sense to say that God really meant that your job ended at their spirit and heart, and he has purposefully left you inadequate to influence their mind. God didn't just forget to include school in his biblical plan for child development; it was not needed because he created the home. You are adequate, and fully equipped by God, to meet all your child's developmental needs through your home.

Sally and I have come to the place where we can honestly say that there is no distinction in our homeschool between home and school; we are living to learn and learning to live all at the same time. That is what should happen in a home. Is WholeHearted Learning a formula to make that happen? No! It is simply a lens through which to plan and evaluate what is happening in your home. It is based on biblical principles, but there is no biblical formula for building a Christian home or for home education. WholeHearted Learning is really just a relational process of loving God and loving your children (and loving books!). In fact, like the Christian life, most of the process of building a Christian home, or of homeschooling for that matter, is simply a matter of walking daily in the power of the Holy Spirit, praying for wisdom, and stepping out in faith. That is what will define your home as a Christian home—that you, with God's help, are nurturing, discipling, and educating your children at home for Christ.

*   *   *

Clay Clarkson is director of Whole Heart Ministries, a non-profit family ministry he founded with Sally in 1994 to encourage and equip Christian parents to raise wholehearted children for Christ. He is the author or editor of numerous books and resources, including *Educating the WholeHearted Child, Our 24 Family Ways,* and *Heartfelt Discipline.*

Clarkson also edits and publishes reprints of public domain works through Whole Heart Press. He is a graduate of Denver Seminary, has ministered full-time since college, and is also a Christian songwriter, singer, and worship leader.

The Clarksons live in Monument, Colorado, and have home-schooled their four children from the beginning.